SCANDAL IN THE CHURCH

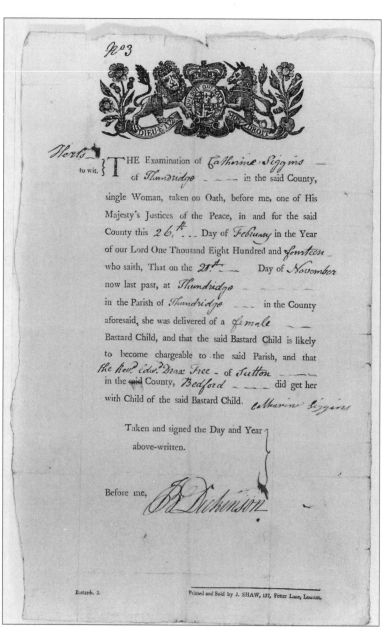

No 3

Herts
to wit.

THE Examination of *Catharine Siggins* — of *Thundridge* _ _ _ _ in the said County, single Woman, taken on Oath, before me, one of His Majesty's Justices of the Peace, in and for the said County this *26th* _ _ Day of *February* in the Year of our Lord One Thousand Eight Hundred and *fourteen* _ who saith, That on the *21st* _ _ Day of *November* now last past, at *Thundridge* _ _ _ _ _ in the Parish of *Thundridge* _ _ _ in the County aforesaid, she was delivered of a *female* _ _ _ Bastard Child, and that the said Bastard Child is likely to become chargeable to the said Parish, and that *the Revd Edwd Drax Free* _ of *Sutton* _ _ _ in the ~~said~~ County, *Bedford* _ _ _ did get her with Child of the said Bastard Child. *Catharine Siggins*

Taken and signed the Day and Year above-written.

Before me, *B. Dickinson*

Bastards. 3.   Printed and Sold by J. SHAW, 137, Fetter Lane, London.

1 A magistrate's examination of Catharine Siggins, 1814.
(*Lambeth Palace Library*)

SCANDAL
IN THE CHURCH

Dr Edward Drax Free, 1764–1843

R. B. Outhwaite

THE HAMBLEDON PRESS

LONDON AND RIO GRANDE

Published by The Hambledon Press 1997
102 Gloucester Avenue, London NW1 8HX (UK)
PO Box 162, Rio Grande, Ohio 45674 (USA)

ISBN 1 85285 165 1

A description of this book is available from
the British Library and from the Library of Congress

Typeset by Carnegie Publishing Ltd, 18 Maynard St, Preston
Printed on acid-free paper and bound in Great Britain by
Cambridge University Press

Contents

Illustrations

Text Illustrations

Acknowledgements

The authors and publisher are grateful to the following for permission to reproduce illustrations: Bedfordshire Record Office, 4 (p. 37), 5 (p. 59); Ann Brady, pl. III; the Syndics of Cambridge University Library, 2 (p. 17), 3 (p. 21), 8 (p. 103), pls I, II, IX, X, XI; Lambeth Palace Library, 1 (p. ii), 9 (p. 105); Henry Outhwaite, 7 (p. 66); the Archives Department of the Royal Free Hospital, 10 (p. 120). Other photographs are the author's.

Foreword

A S SUCCESSIVE EDITORS of the *News of the World* have long
appreciated, everyone likes to read about disreputable clergymen. The petty delinquencies of ordinary people are too common
and too depressing to make a good story. But when fleshly weak-
nesses are juxtaposed with the high ideals of the clerical office, even
the most sordid tale of human inadequacy can take on an irresistible
piquancy. Over the centuries there has been no shortage of delinquent English clergyman whose escapades have captured the public
imagination. The genre was established in the 1640s, when the
reforming zeal of the Parliamentarians led to the publication of such
works as John White's *The First Century of Scandalous, Malignant
Priests Admitted into Benefices by the Prelates* (1643). This sad collection
of drunkards, fornicators and adulterers set the pattern for many
later narratives.

Now we have another addition to this dubious pantheon: the
Reverend Dr Edward Drax Free. In his *The History of St. John's
College, Oxford, 1598–1860* (1958), Dr W. C. Costin described Free's
career as one of 'disgrace to himself, the College, and the Church'.
This was no understatement. Narrowly avoiding expulsion for his
violent and contumacious behaviour as a Fellow of St John's, Free
was presented in 1808 by his misguided college to the benefice of
Sutton in Bedfordshire. As incumbent of that unfortunate parish
for the next twenty-one years, he kept his pigs in the churchyard
and his cattle in the church porch, sold the lead off the church
roof, refused to christen or bury his parishioners and fathered at

least five illegitimate children. In a work of lucid and painstaking scholarship, Brian Outhwaite has reconstructed the complicated history of the six years of litigation which proved necessary before the miscreant could be evicted from his living.

It is an absorbing tale, fascinatingly narrated. Legal historians will value it for the light it throws upon the church courts in the early nineteenth century and their relationship to the common law jurisdiction: whether or not Free's case led directly to the Royal Commission on Ecclesiastical Courts of 1830 and the Church Discipline Act of 1840, it was certainly a prominent feature in the background to those measures. Social historians will appreciate the tale of Edward Drax Free for the way in which it illustrates such varied matters as the role of the village squire and the vulnerability of female domestic servants. Anyone who likes a piece of historical detection well told will relish this pre-Victorian miniature, the unhappy story of a man who had been at college with Jane Austen's brother.

Corpus Christi College, Oxford   Keith Thomas

Preface

I T WAS OVER TWENTY YEARS AGO, whilst pursuing an interest in the later history of the English church courts, that I read Charles Coote's *The Practice of the Ecclesiastical Courts*, a mid Victorian guide to legal procedures in these clerical tribunals, and there came across 'The Office of the Judge Promoted by Montagu Burgoyne, Esquire, against the Reverend Edward Drax Free, Doctor in Divinity'.[1] This was offered as an example of how to frame 'Articles against a clergyman for incontinence', but the list of thirty-one 'Articles' with which Free was charged were so many and so various, stretching as they did over nineteen pages of Coote's text, that I was half convinced that he had invented the case so as to provide as comprehensive a list of clerical sins as possible. It was much later, when working through English law reports, that I discovered that the case was a real one, and not an invention. I now realise that Coote was able to print this document because he was one of the 'Condelegates' or Judges appointed to consider certain issues when Free appealed his case in 1826 to the High Court of Delegates.[2] Two years ago it dawned on me that Sutton, the village in which this extraordinary series of events took place, was only a short

---

1 H. C. Coote, *The Practice of the Ecclesiastical Courts* (London, 1847), pp. 158–76.

2 The Articles printed by Coote, however, were the 'reformed' ones, omitting, for example, the fourth and twenty-first of them. The full set, including those subsequently dropped, is printed as Appendix 4, see below, pp. 151–67.

distance from my home in Cambridge, lying as it does just over the border in neighbouring Bedfordshire. A visit to the village, and sight of its picturesque church and handsome rectory, confirmed my desire to find out more about the case and the events surrounding it.

My pursuit of Dr Free has led to enquiries in many places. I should particularly like to thank Melanie Barber and her assistants at Lambeth Palace Library, where my enquiries began, and Dr Malcolm Vale, the Keeper of the Muniments at St John's College, Oxford, who found letters that had escaped my notice on an earlier visit to the College. In addition I am grateful for the often considerable help given by the archivists of the Bedfordshire Record Office, the British Library, the Essex Record Office, the Hampshire Record Office, the Lincolnshire Archives, the Northumberland Record Office, the Oxfordshire Archives, the Somerset Archive and Record Service and the West Sussex Record Office. I must thank also Lynn Botelho who searched several sources in the Bodleian Library, Oxford, for me; Ian Ritchie, of the National Portrait Gallery, for information on portraits; Stephen Coppel, who guided my search through Thomas Rowlandson's prints; Ann Brady, who supplied the Victorian photograph of Sutton Rectory, and who kindly showed me around Dr Free's former residence; and David Hool for great efforts on my behalf, not the least of which was a willingness to penetrate the thickets of the records of the Court of King's Bench in the Public Record Office.

I have attempted, when quoting from the documents these various archives yielded, to retain contemporary spelling and capitalisation, but have sometimes altered the punctuation for reasons of clarity.

Many others have helped me in various ways: Vic Gatrell, Boyd Hilton and David Thompson gave bibliographical guidance; Michael Prichard offered invaluable help in response to a stream of legal queries; and Stephen Waddams gave me the benefit of his considerable knowledge of ecclesiastical court procedures in the early nineteenth century. Piers Brendon and Jacqueline Watson read some early drafts of this work. Louise Foxcroft scrutinised the final version, constantly making me rethink my position in relation to Dr Free. Martin Sheppard has once again made publishing a book with Hambledon Press a pleasure. Finally, I must thank Sir Keith Thomas for agreeing to my request that he should write a Foreword: it seemed peculiarly fitting that one of St John's most distinguished Fellows should pass judgement on one of that Oxford College's least distinguished sons.

Abbreviations

BL	British Library, London
BRO	Bedfordshire Record Office, Bedford
CJ	*Journals of the House of Commons*
DNB	*Dictionary of National Biography*
ERO	Essex Record Office, Chelmsford
HRO	Hampshire Record Office, Winchester
LA	Lincolnshire Archives, Lincoln
LJ	*Journals of the House of Lords*
LPL	Lambeth Palace Library, London
NRO	Northumberland Record Office, Newcastle
OA	Oxfordshire Archives, Oxford
PP	*Parliamentary Papers*
PRO	Public Record Office, London
QSR	Quarter Session Records
WCA	Westminster City Archives, London
WSRO	West Sussex Record Office, Chichester

I

Origins and Oxford

IN JUNE 1825 an extraordinary and lengthy petition was tabled in Parliament. It came from Montagu Burgoyne, the great-uncle of Sir John Montagu Burgoyne, the latter being the principal landowner within the village of Sutton in Bedfordshire.[1] Describing himself as Churchwarden of Sutton, the petitioner complained on behalf of himself and other parishioners of that small community about the delays that they were then experiencing in the legal prosecution of the clergyman who since 1808 had been their Rector, Edward Drax Free, Doctor in Divinity of the University of Oxford. They complained of his 'Incontinence, Drunkenness, profane and indecent Language, the Omissions and Negligence, the Extortions and Abuses in his Discharge of his holy Office'. After detailing some of the offences alleged against him – 'alleged' for nothing by this stage had been resolved in a court of law – the document went on to say:

> that if the Parish of Sutton had been compelled to hire a Person for the express Purpose of dishonoring the Church of England in its most sacred Offices, of weakening the Attachment of its Members, and of bringing Doubts and Discouragements on the Truth or Value of Religion itself, their Choice could not have been more judiciously directed than towards the Clergyman to whose Outrages and Contaminations they have been thus cruelly abandoned ...[2]

1 On the Burgoynes, see Chapter 4 below, pp. 57–73.
2 *Journals of the House of Lords* [hereafter *LJ*], 57, pp. 1110–11.

Who was this man that provoked such passionate vituperation? What exactly were the charges levelled against him? Were they justified? And, if they were, why was it proving so difficult to bring him to justice? When four years later he was eventually sentenced, a leading article in *The Times* commented 'This FREE is a terrible fellow, indeed', and it went on to ask, 'Where did he come from? Where was he educated?'[3]

Edward Drax Free came from a clerical family. His father, John Free, was an Oxford man, born in that city and educated there.[4] Admitted as a fifteen-year-old 'plebeian' to Christ Church in 1727, John Free proceeded to the B.A. degree in 1730, the M.A. in 1733, and acted also as Chaplain to that famous body.[5] At some later point he transferred to Hertford College. It was there, in 1744, that he took, at the age of thirty-three, the B.D. and D.D. degrees. Before this, however, he had become Vicar of Runcorn in Cheshire, a living he held from 1740 to 1756, and in 1742 was also appointed Lecturer in the London parish of St James Garlickhithe. Numerous other positions came the way of this vigorous preacher and polemicist, though he complained later in life that there was little financial reward in any of them. In 1746 he married and a year later was elected Master of Queen Elizabeth's Grammar School in St

---

3 *The Times*, 26 June 1829, p. 2.

4 John Free's father, another John, was an Oxford watchmaker who had a prosperous business until he fell out of favour after 1715 because of his support of George I. He acquired the nickname of 'Skinny Free', not because of his meanness, but because he was 'a very great Whig' who 'wished all the Tories throughout the World were flea'd, and their Skins hung up upon Trees, and their Heads upon Pinnacles'. He died in 1721, at the age of forty-three, leaving a wife and three children. See *Remarks and Collections of Thomas Hearne*, ix, ed. H. E. Salter (Oxford, 1914), p. 90; and J. Free, *A Volume of Sermons Preached before the University of Oxford* (London, 1750), pp. xiv–xvi.

5 This account of Dr John Free is based on John Nichols, *Literary Anecdotes of the Eighteenth Century* (London, 1812), v, pp. 687–95; J. Foster, *Alumni Oxonienses* (Oxford, 1888), ii, p. 492; and genealogical information kindly supplied by David Hool.

Saviour's, Southwark. He was a reluctant schoolmaster, regarding the occupation as one that sapped his vitality as a preacher. The preface that he wrote for a collection of his sermons published in 1750 spoke disparagingly of the profession:

> For, with regard to the contemptible TRADE of School-teaching, the common refuge upon these Occasions, it is the worst suited of any to the Purpose, and Business of a Clergyman. It has in it all the Tameness, Meanness, and Confinement of the lowest Servility; and is so far from being consistent with their Studies, that, though it may advance the Learning of a Boy, it is nothing but Destruction and Distraction to the Learning of a Man.[6]

Soon after this, in 1751, his wife Elizabeth died, but Free had by now acquired a taste for the married state and he quickly married again. Elizabeth and his second wife, Mary, produced between them a succession of children, one of whom died in 1754 and another in 1757. Meanwhile, in 1756, Free relinquished his living at Run-corn to become Vicar of East Coker in Somerset. Neither of his clerical livings probably saw very much of him. Both his dead children were buried at St Mary's church in Newington, Surrey, and between 1761 and 1767 four other children were baptised in that same church or in neighbouring Lambeth. The first of these newcomers was John, replacing an earlier John who had died in 1757. He arrived in 1761 and was followed a year later by Beckwith Dodwell Free, whom we shall briefly encounter again. The elder Free's third son, Edward Drax, was born two days before Christmas in 1764 and baptised a month later. A further son arrived in 1767, but he died soon after birth.

John Free, the elder, survived to the age of eighty, dying in his chambers at Lyons Inn, London, in 1791.[7] It is likely that he had little wealth to pass on to his younger sons.[8] He was complaining

---

6   Free, *Volume of Sermons*, p. viii.
7   *Gentleman's Magazine*, 61 (1791), p. 876.
8   A will has not been located.

about the 'Ill-distribution of Preferment' as early as 1750, and his bitterness was likely to have increased with the passing years, doomed as he saw it 'to the never-ending Confinement and Fatigue of a public School'.[9] Three years before his death he wrote a lengthy letter to John Moore, the Archbishop of Canterbury, complaining that his career had been blighted by a series of events: the death of the Prince of Wales, the opposition of the Duke of Newcastle and his supporters, and the inability of the three Bishops from whom he had sought patronage to offer him anything more than a vicarage worth about £70 a year 'to struggle with the world, and bring up a family'. Warming to his task, and describing himself as 'Emeritus Miles Ecclesiae Anglicanae', he complained that his situation was worse than that of a Chelsea Pensioner:

> for they are supported by the Military Establishment, whilst a Clergyman, whose writings, preaching, and behaviour, have been irreproachable, is turned over to another profession – to ask for bread.[10]

Apart from the extraordinarily lengthy list of sermons and tracts that Free published, he also composed and left among his papers his own epitaph. If it was intended for his tomb, the latter must have been planned on a truly pharaonic scale for the epitaph runs to over eighty lines of Latin text. It begins – in the translation thoughtfully provided by the *Gentleman's Magazine* for its readers:

Here lies buried
John Free, D.D.
Of the University of Oxford;
A native of that city;
Of both the father:
For at the time of his decease
There was not an older citizen,
Nor, of the University, a Doctor.

9 Free, *Volume of Sermons*, pp. viii–ix.
10 Nichols, *Literary Anecdotes*, pp. 688–91.

This man lived in vain,
For he laboured in vain!
Desired no more than
The moderate necessaries of life;
But failed to procure even these,
Either for himself or family.[11]

Why John Free decided to christen his son 'Edward Drax' we do not know for certain, but it seems probable that he was named after Edward Drax, a contemporary of his at Hertford College who later became the Member of Parliament for Wareham in Dorset.[12] Like his elder brother Beckwith, Edward was educated at Merchant Taylors' School in London and, again like Beckwith, he secured one of the many tied Sir Thomas White Scholarships to St John's College, Oxford, the two institutions being linked through the thirty-seven Fellowships appropriated to the school through the munificence of Sir Thomas White, the wealthy mid sixteenth-century London merchant who founded the College.[13] Beckwith, however, left St John's in 1780, the year before Edward arrived. Hart, the compiler of the School's biographical dictionary, wrote that he 'resigned his Fellowship by order of the President (Samuel Dennis)'.[14] St John's Register, however, simply records that 'Beckwith Dodwell Free having transmitted to the President his Resignation of his Scholarship with the Consent of his Father

11   *Gentleman's Magazine*, 61 (1791), pp. 967–68, 1048. The Latin epitaph was published in the October issue, and translated for the benefit of most of its readers in the following November issue. It is reproduced in full as Appendix 1, see below, pp. 141–43.
12   Sir L. Namier and J. Brooke, *The House of Commons* (London, 1964), i, p. 340. In a letter written in 1788 Free comments on information passed to him by Drax, with whom he had obviously kept up contact, Nichols, *Literary Anecdotes*, p. 688. Four members of the Drax family are listed amongst the subscribers to his 1750 volume of sermons.
13   J. Foster, *Oxford Men and their Colleges* (Oxford and London, 1893), p. 466; Anon., *Merchant Taylors' School: Its Origin, History and Present Surroundings* (Oxford, 1929), pp. 35, 38; *Merchant Taylors' School Register, 1561–1934*, ed. E. P. Hart (London, 1936), no pagination.
14   Hart, *School Register*, no pagination.

annexed, it was accordingly declared void'.[15] Given that within a year Beckwith was enrolled as a student at Lincoln's Inn, it may well be that John Free had decided upon a more lucrative career for his eldest son than the church that he considered, rightly or wrongly, had treated him so shabbily.

We should remember that, whatever the ambitions of its intellectual leaders, Oxford University in the second half of the eighteenth century still performed its two principal and highly traditional tasks. The first was that it prepared young men for a career in the Church of England. The second was that it served as a finishing school for the children of the wealthy. 'Boating, hunting, shooting, fishing – these formed in times of yore the chief amusement of the Oxford scholar', wrote a St John's contemporary of Dr Free looking back on his own undergraduate days.[16] Like its East Anglian rival, Cambridge, it presented the majority of undergraduates with few intellectual challenges. Although candidates for bachelor degrees at Oxford were supposed to attend public disputations and lectures in preparation for the oral examinations that were to set their proficiency, the latter were in the words of a recent historian 'banal and stereotyped'.[17] The same situation prevailed for the disputations that were part of the examination for the M.A. degree, the six lectures that formed the remaining part being customarily offered to empty rooms. One Magdalen man confessed in 1798 to not preparing his own lectures, admitting that he simply read out aloud 'those which had been for many years almost invariably taken into the Schools by our Men'.[18]

College life appears initially to have presented few obstacles to the youthful Edward Drax Free, the younger son destined for the church. By 1784 he had become a Fellow of St John's, taking his

15 St John's College, Oxford, Register, vii, fol. 534.
16 T. F. Dibdin (matriculated 1793), cited in W. C. Costin, *The History of St John's College, Oxford, 1598–1860* (Oxford, 1958), p. 227.
17 L. S. Sutherland, 'The Curriculum', in *The History of the University of Oxford*, v, *The Eighteenth Century*, ed., L. S. Sutherland and L. G. Mitchell (Oxford, 1986), p. 471.
18 Ibid., p. 482.

B.A. the following year and the M.A. degree in 1789. It was expected of most Oxford Fellows that they should proceed to Holy Orders, and should take degrees in the Faculty of Divinity. The formal requirements here were hardly more severe than those for the B.A. and M.A., the principal ones being the passage of specified periods of time since obtaining the M.A., attendance at University lectures that were frequently non-existent, the delivery of certain sermons or lectures, and the payment of the appropriate fees.[19] Edward Drax Free duly proceeded along the prescribed route, taking the B.D. degree in 1794. Five years later, however, we encounter the first recorded sign of the difficulties that were later to accompany him. The Bishop of Winchester, the College Visitor, had apparently to persuade Free into 'a proper submission to the authority of the College' before St John's would present him for his Doctor in Divinity degree.[20] Before this College offices had started to come his way: in 1792 he was Dean of Arts and in 1796 he was appointed Curate of Northmoor and Dean of Divinity.[21] Appointments to College lectureships followed, and in 1801 he was presented to the Vicarage of St Giles, Oxford, a College living that he was permitted to hold without resigning his Fellowship.[22] This appointment marked the end of whatever benevolence the College was prepared to extend to him: from that point onwards he held none of those College offices and lectureships that normally circulated annually in the Fellowship, and personal relationships within the fraternity became distinctly sour.

Here one must admit some of the limitations of our evidence relating to Edward Drax Free. No portrait of him, for example, has been located. Whether he was tall or short, fat or thin is not known. He left few personal letters and there is no diary. We rely

19   Ibid., pp. 486–89.
20   Foster, *Alumni Oxonienses*, p. 492; Hampshire Record Office, Winchester [hereafter HRO], 21 M 65/J7, letter of 25 January 1808.
21   St John's College, Oxford, Register, viii, 1795–1834, pp. 28–29; Costin, *History of St John's*, p. 228.
22   Ibid., pp. 55, 64, 80.

largely, therefore, on what others said about him and on the impressions left by his own conduct. Witnesses who testified against him in the late 1820s commented on his red face and the violence of his temperament. 'His manner is coarse, rude, quarrelsome, and at times very abusive', said one; 'a very cross looking man', said another; 'an insane man ... violent and quarrelsome', said a third.[23] These were not late onset characteristics; they were qualities that his colleagues at St John's and his parishioners at St Giles's had recognised a quarter of a century earlier. He was, to say the very least, an extraordinarily difficult man.

The Churchwardens of St Giles presented complaints to the Archdeacon of Oxford in 1806 that their Vicar, Dr Free, had so far offered no account of the distribution of the 'sacraments money' and indeed positively refused to offer any such account.[24] The following year saw the parish vestry complaining that 'Dr Free had forcibly taken the Book of Benefactions and other Books belonging to the said Parish'.[25] Three months later they again presented him to the Archdeacon, complaining that:

> the Vicar still refuses the Church Warden to have anything to do with the Sacrament Money. He has also taken several Books out of the Parish Chest, which he refuses to return. He also marries Persons neither of whom have resided in his Parish. He also has omitted to pray for sick Persons, although required so to do.[26]

Even after his departure from the parish these complaints from the Churchwardens continued, for Dr Free failed to return the 'Book of Benefactions and other paper concerning the Parish', as well as the key to the parish chest.[27]

23 Lambeth Palace Library, London [hereafter LPL], H427/56, fos 65v, 105r, 128v.
24 Oxfordshire Archives, Oxford [hereafter OA], Archdeaconry Papers, c 91, nos 204, 207.
25 OA, St Giles, Vestry Minute Book, p. 24.
26 OA, Archdeaconry Papers, c 91, no. 209.
27 Ibid., no. 211.

This was behaviour his College had cause to recognise. In January 1808 Dr Marlow, the President of St John's, and five senior Fellows sent a lengthy and remarkable letter to the Bishop of Winchester, whose function it was, as Visitor to the College, to settle disputes and maintain harmony in that body. They begged the Bishop to intercede and persuade Dr Free to submit himself to authority because they were on the point of expelling him from their society. They wished, however, not to be driven to this:

> because he is senior to most of us, because his views in Life depend on the Preferment he may obtain from the Society, and because we cannot but regard him with pity, his Judgment being perverted by a temper naturally bad, and he having no friend in the Society to advise him.

They went on to point out that 'the Temper of Dr Free is such, that he has not of late years been elected to any office of Trust or Discipline' and that 'after many instances of verbal abuse towards different officers of the College, he was on the 28th of October 1806 guilty of violence toward the Bursar'.

This act of violence was investigated and the truth of it established by the appropriate College body, which as a punishment deprived Free of his 'Commons' – his meals – and his stipend for one week. The statutes of the College decreed that such punishments had to be entered by the offender in the Vice-President's Register, so that on repetition of the offence the punishment could be increased by stages leading perhaps to his eventual expulsion. This was the beginning of the richly comic episode of the Vice-President's Register.[28]

Dr Free, predictably enough, refused to make the required entry, causing the College to invoke another statute depriving him of Commons worth 3s. 6d. a week until he eventually submitted himself. This apparently only caused his behaviour to become even more intolerable, leading to his verbally abusing the President at a

---

28 An alternative account is to be found in Costin, *History of St John's*, pp. 228–30, though the dating is there confused.

public dinner in October 1807. Those present were so scandalised by this incident that Free was called upon to attend a special meeting of the College officers arranged for 26 October in the Vice-President's rooms.

The summons to attend this meeting was delivered to him by the Porter of the College, but Free failed to appear. So a further punishment of deprivation of Commons and pension was imposed. To ensure that entries in the record would be made in the appropriate Register, the latter was delivered personally to Dr Free by the College Porter. The Register failed to reappear. The College officers requested its return through another note carried by the long-suffering Porter, who reported that Dr Free told him 'to bring him no more Messages for he would not receive them'. He then apparently threw the note out of his room. He did, however, tell the Porter that he had left the Register some time ago outside the door of his rooms, and that he had not seen it since.

A further meeting of the officers took place on 20 November, leading to a note, carried this time by the Under-Butler, ordering Free to return the Register on or before the 26 November or face the consequences of his contumacy. The note came back unopened, Free complaining that he was too ill to receive it. Back the note went, but still the Register failed to reappear.

At a routine meeting on 30 November 1806, called to elect College officers, the President specifically asked Free, who was present on this occasion, where the Register was, and whether he intended to return it. Free recapitulated that 'he had put it out of his Room into a Passage and had not seen it since', adding also that he had failed to open the last note sent by the President.

Two days later the President called a special meeting of the officers to discuss the whole matter. They resolved to lay the matter before the Bishop as a last step before the likely expulsion from the College of a senior Fellow, one 'who in all Probability will very soon be a Candidate for Preferment from it'.[29] It was this

29 HRO, 21 M 65/J7.

decision that lay behind the long letter of 25 January 1808 addressed by the officers of the College to the Bishop.

Quickly responding to their pleas for intercession, the Bishop agreed to intervene and affirmed his aim of reconciliation, writing 'My intention is to appeal to his feelings of Interest and Character and to the love of Peace which becomes him as Clergyman'.[30] A rough draft of the Bishop's cautious and overly optimistic letter to Free survives in the Winchester archives. It urged 'the line of amicable and concordant behaviour, which is due from you', and, dripping with oil destined for troubled waters, exhorted and entreated him 'to consider how much more consistent it would be with your Character as a Clergyman, and a Member of the College, to respect with gratitude the Founder's rule'. Preceded by rather veiled warnings about the consequences 'to one so highly advanced in the Society', the Bishop suggested either the rediscovery of the old Register or the signing of a newly-provided one.[31]

How, or indeed whether, Dr Free eventually came to heel in this affair we do not know. As far as the College was concerned a miracle occurred. In the summer of 1808 Dr Samuel Kettilby, Professor of Geometry at Gresham College in London and Rector of Sutton in Bedfordshire, died at the age of seventy-three, thus freeing a College living.[32] This, in accordance with standard practice, was offered to the Fellows in order of their seniority, and in October 1808 Dr Free accepted the College's nomination to it.[33] It was not the richest of livings, but it was a modestly comfortable one. Some years later Dr Free reckoned that Kettilby derived an income, net of taxes, of just over £250 a year from Sutton, with most of it coming from a rent charge on the Burgoyne properties that was

30 Ibid., letter of 13 February 1808.
31 Ibid., draft letter of 15 February 1808.
32 *Gentleman's Magazine*, 78 (1808), p. 657.
33 St John's College, Register, viii, 1795–1834, p. 153. Dr Free later asserted, in his 1833 petition to the College Visitor, that the living was turned down by two of his seniors – 'Dr Freeman and Dr Forbs' – because of the 'treatment and encroachments the former Rector, Dr Kettilby, had received from the Burgoyne family', HRO, 21 M 65/J7.

offered in exchange for the abandonment of the Rector's tithes at the time of the enclosure by Act of Parliament of Sutton's arable fields in 1741.[34]

Dr Free's acceptance of Sutton must have persuaded the College, and its President in particular, of the powers of prayer. Six months earlier the long-suffering Marlow had written to the Bishop of Winchester confessing that he had always tried to help Free, 'in the sincere hope that I might prevent the Ruin of a Man I have always pitied, and enable him to quit the Society without disgrace'.[35] President Marlow's hopes must have been quickly dashed, if only by the financial irregularities that soon came to the College's attention.

St John's experience of living with Free, let alone that of his tenure as Vicar of St Giles, should have alerted his superiors to his potential limitations as a parish priest, but as far as the College was concerned Dr Free was more than ripe for preferment. It made every effort to ease his transition. In October 1808 it voted him £50 from the 'Winterslow Fund' to enable him to replace a brick floor in the Rectory parlour with a wooden one. In November 1809 he was promised a further £50 from the same source and £100 from the 'Promotion Fund' towards the improvement of the Rectory. This came after Mr Hudson, an Oxford builder who was employed as the College's surveyor, went with Free to Sutton to assess the cost of 'dilapidations' arising from the previous tenancy and to estimate the cost of improving the property. The dilapidations were assessed at £177, a sum which it was thought Free duly received from Kettilby's executors; the proposed improvements were estimated at between three and four hundred pounds.

Only £50 of the £200 promised by the College was paid to Dr

---

34 This rent, which varied in accordance with the price of corn, was paid quarterly by the Burgoynes to the Rector. Not all tithes were suppressed. Certain specified pasture closes were excepted from the agreement, and these were to become tithable if ever tilled. St John's College, MSS L10 (v), L11 (i).

35 HRO, 21 M 65/J7.

Free, because it must quickly have become apparent to the College officers that the money that he was receiving was not being used for its intended purposes and also that he was also raising money by other means. In March 1811 the College wrote to the Bishop of Lincoln enquiring whether he or his officials had given the Rector permission to cut down trees at Sutton. The Bishop replied that not only had no such application been received, but if it had been he would have appointed a person to ascertain whether there were any trees in a fit state to be cut down for 'useful and necessary repairs or improvement of the premises'. He emphasised that incumbents did not have the right to cut down and sell timber, using the purchase money to repair buildings. The timber itself had actually to be used on the premises. If Dr Free had been exceeding his powers, then the patrons must proceed against him as having committed 'waste', and he advised the College to take legal counsel on this.[36]

No immediate action appears to have been taken by the College, until in June 1812 they received a request from a solicitor employed by Free, asking for the remaining £150 to be paid to him. Their reply was that the remainder would be handed over when the College surveyor had certified that the repairs and alterations were finished 'according to the Plan'.

In October 1812 Mr Hudson made his way to Sutton where 'Dr Free ... refused him admission into the House', so that the surveyor could not ascertain what repairs or improvements had been undertaken. He made enquiries in nearby Biggleswade, however, where he learnt that very little work had been done in the Rectory and that only a few fences around the glebe had been repaired. When Hudson was previously in Sutton, moreover, there had been a copse near the Rectory full of fine young timber. By 1812 most of this had been chopped down and taken away. The man who bought this timber from Dr Free admitted to the surveyor that 'they were the finest thriving Trees he had ever seen, and that it was a shame

36 St John's College, MS L10 (13 March 1811).

to cut them'. Hudson believed that there had been between two and three hundred oaks, elms, ashes and alders, worth about £200, and now only about a dozen of the smallest were left. In addition to this, Hudson thought that from twelve to fifteen large ash and fir trees, worth about £60, had disappeared from the churchyard. Fifteen ash trees, taken from other parts of the glebe, were lying by the roadside waiting to be carted away.

In November 1812 the College wrote to Free telling him that the £150 previously promised could not be paid until the surveyor had established that the proposed works had been properly undertaken. He was also warned that the College was taking legal advice as to whether it could obtain financial compensation in respect of the trees that he had disposed of.

The Rector characteristically took no notice of this letter, with the consequence that in February 1813 the College duly rescinded the order voting him £150. St John's decided also to seek legal opinion and was advised that the ecclesiastical court of the diocese was the proper forum for such a grievance but that it could not obtain financial damages in that court.[37]

These activities alone would no doubt have kept Free's name circulating at Oxford dinner tables. Worse, however, was to follow.

---

37 The whole episode is related 'For the Opinion of Mr Abbott', of the Inner Temple, in St John's College, MS L10 (iii).

2

Sutton and the Housekeepers

D R FREE was clearly an accident waiting to happen and, despite the hopes of the President of St John's College, the place where it occurred was Sutton, to the living of which he had been presented in October 1808. The 'accident' took the form not of a single event, but of a sequence of events, a gradual accumulation of insults to that community's inhabitants, leading them eventually to seek his prosecution and removal.

Sutton is a village situated about a mile and a half to the south of the small Bedfordshire market town of Potton, lying off the modern road that runs from Potton to Biggleswade. The census of 1811, taken not long after Free's arrival, gave its population as 301, made up of fifty-six families, fifty-two of which were 'chiefly employed in agriculture'. By 1831 its population had grown to 386: of its seventy-two families, sixty-nine were employed in agriculture.[1] This latter snapshot fits the picture of Sutton described by the witnesses who deposed in 1828–29 against Dr Free at his trial in the Court of Arches. William Coxall, one of Sutton's larger farmers, was amongst these witnesses. There were altogether in the parish, Coxall stated, ten farms and nine farmers. All of them were tenants of the Burgoyne family, who owned all of the parish's 2230 acres except for the Rectory and the glebe land attached to it, which

---

1 *Abstracts of Population Returns for MDCCCXI* (House of Commons, 1812), xi, *County of Bedford*, p. 1; *Abstract of the Answers and Returns* (House of Commons, 1833).

amounted to thirty-two acres in all.[2] Another witness, James Steers, a
coachman from Potton, described these farmers as 'large and
respectable'. The remaining population consisted principally of labourers and cottagers who were, or had been, employed on these
farms, although the community included also a blacksmith and a
carpenter-wheelwright. It also housed some retired servants of the
Burgoynes. The place, stated another of these farmers, 'is a very
comfortable one and the inhabitants are well kept as labourers'.
The village had no public house and it appears to have lacked a
general shop.[3] Most of the inhabitants of Sutton would have walked
or ridden the mile or so to Potton to purchase their necessaries.
Others would have made their way to the more substantial town
of Biggleswade. By 1831 Biggleswade had a population of over
3000, and it was only about a mile further from Sutton than Potton.
It lay also on the Great North Road and consequently had good
stage coach connections with London.

If, as seems likely, Dr Free first approached Sutton from the
direction of Biggleswade, then All Saints church at the west end
of the village would have been the first building to have attracted
his attention. Situated on a mound, high above the level of the
road, surrounded by its walls, this ancient church built of stone and
cobbles must have pleased all but the most jaundiced eye.

Hard against the east wall of the churchyard lay the Rectory, an
appealing mixture of early half-timbering and Queen Anne, with
an elegant stuccoed front. Behind, and to the north and east of the
church and the Rectory, lay Sutton Park, the home of the Burgoyne
family, whose box pews and burial monuments dominate the
interior of the church. 'The Family Mansion', the *Gentleman's
Magazine* informed its readers in 1810, 'is a large modern building,

2 LPL, H427/56, fol. 63r. These acreages are taken from the agreement
   made in 1838 for the commutation of the remaining tithes, St John's
   College, MS L11(i).
3 LPL, H427/56, fos 33r, 54r ('there is a blacksmith and a carpenter'), 63r,
   71r ('a smith and one small shopkeeper, a chandler'), 115v ('a
   wheelwright and a smith'). I have deduced from all this that there was
   a blacksmith and a carpenter-wheelwright's shop in the village.

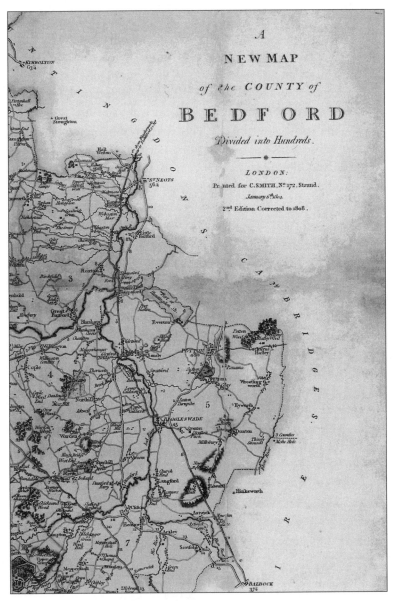

2. Section of 1804 map of Bedfordshire
(*Cambridge University Library*)

seated in the middle of a small but beautiful park.' Although Sutton Park was easily the largest and most gracious building in this attractively situated parish, the Rector occupied the next largest and next most imposing dwelling in the community.

Its very size must have presented Dr Free with a problem, since it needed to be maintained. He had no wife, and life as a Fellow of St John's College would not have developed his domestic talents. His successor as Rector of Sutton, Charles Dethick Blyth, was married, and the 1851 census reveals that besides his wife the Rectory housed an errand boy, a groom, a house maid, a waiting maid and, heading the list of servants, a forty-seven year old housekeeper.[4] Whilst Dr Free employed a succession of handymen to do jobs around the house, and to help him tend his animals and his farmland, none of them ever lived in. The only servants who slept beneath his roof were female ones. There were, indeed, a succession of housekeepers, mostly young, but only ever one at a time. Their stories, revealed principally but not entirely in the depositions they made during Dr Free's trial in 1828–29, are the subject of this chapter.[5]

Maria Crook was the first of his female employees. Born in nearby Potton, she was twenty-five years old when in 1810 she came to work for Dr Free as his housekeeper. Although this might be thought to be young for such a responsible position, she had already had experience as a servant. At one stage she worked for a Potton family, the Tears, as William Tear, a bricklayer, later attested.[6] When she was aged about nineteen she bettered herself by obtaining employment with local grandees, the Pym family who dwelt at nearby Sandy, and it was Francis Pym who took her to work in the family's London house in Clarges Street, Picadilly. By

---

4 Bedfordshire Record Office, Bedford [hereafter BRO], typescript copy of 1851 household enumeration returns for Sutton.
5 In telling their stories, I have tried to stick to facts that were verified by more than one witness, facts that were sometimes accepted by Dr Free himself.
6 LPL, H427/56, fol. 87v.

1805, however, she had left Pym's employment, and by 1807 had returned to her birthplace, claiming support from the local poor law authorities. This led to her being removed by the Bedfordshire justices back to the parish in which (through her employment with the Pyms) she had acquired a settlement entitling her to such support. So in February 1807 she was ordered to be removed from Potton back to the London parish of St George's, Hanover Square.[7] The lure of her birthplace appears to have drawn her back to Bedfordshire once again, however, for immediately before she entered Free's service she lodged for about two months at the Potton home of Nicholas Brown, another bricklayer, sharing a bed apparently with Brown's young teenage daughter.[8]

When exactly in 1810 she became Dr Free's house-servant we do not know and how long she continued working for him became a matter for dispute. Eighteen years later, when called to testify against the Rector, all she could remember was that it was 'in the winter when she went into his service'.[9] She was certainly working in his house on 7 December 1810 when the Rector violently attacked William Bigg, a Potton shopkeeper, who had called to present a bill.[10] Within three weeks of entering Free's employment she was sleeping with the forty-six year old clergyman, and Maria maintained that thereafter 'she had such connection with him repeatedly'.[11] She alleged that this continued through the seven or eight weeks that she continued to work for him. Her service came to an end, Maria maintained, after they quarrelled over her refusal to take a pill that the Rector wished her to take.[12] This quarrel led to Free physically assaulting her, leading Maria to retaliate in spirited fashion by smashing some of his windows and quitting his service.

7 BRO, P64/13/2/28; Quarter Session Records (hereafter QSR) PUBZ 3/3, p. 24.
8 LPL, H427/56, fol. 37v.
9 Ibid.
10 See below, Chapter 3, pp. 45–46.
11 LPL, H 427/56, fol. 35r and v.
12 Ibid., fol. 38r: perhaps an abortifacient.

Her subsequent history tells us much about the problems faced by poor female domestic servants and the resourcefulness they sometimes displayed in overcoming them. On leaving Dr Free, and at that point not entirely sure that she was pregnant, she went into service in the household of Dr Yates, the Mayor of Bedford.[13] There she began to swell in size, leading her employer and the poor law authorities to question her about her condition. Fearing that she would once again be deported to her parish of settlement in London, she initially denied that she was pregnant. She used the respite she was given to write to Dr Free, offering that if he would make financial provision for her delivery and for the child's maintenance she would not expose him as the father. This strategy did not work, for not only was she discharged by Dr Yates but Dr Free also appears to have complained that Maria was threatening him. It may indeed have been at Free's instigation that she was arrested and brought before her former Bedford employer, acting in his capacity as a Bedford magistrate. On 3 July 1811, as an unmarried pregnant woman, she was formally examined as to her place of settlement, and was again sent off to London. Eight days later she was formally examined by a Middlesex magistrate: she admitted that she was pregnant and swore the child's father was Dr Free, the Rector of Sutton.[14]

It was in the parish workhouse of St George's Hanover Square that Maria was delivered of her child. The baby girl survived for only a few weeks: 'Ann Crook' was baptised on 15 September 1811 and was buried on 26 September.[15] Maria herself was very ill for some time afterwards, but she was discharged from the workhouse

---

13 According to the timetable of events that Maria presented, she could not have been pregnant for more than five weeks, making her uncertainty over her condition highly plausible. Also, if she had been certain she was pregnant she would surely not have entered the employment of a magistrate such as Dr Yates.

14 LPL, H427/56, fol. 38r and v; H427/55; BRO, QSR PUBZ 3/3, p. 24.

15 Westminster City Archives, London [hereafter WCA], records of St George's Hanover Square, Baptism Register 6, and Burial Register 92.

3. Engraving of All Saints, Sutton, from *Gentleman's Magazine* (1810)
(*Cambridge University Library*)

on 15 October 1811.[16] Some time after this she made her way back
to Bedford where she eventually entered the service of a Captain
Wilson. There she remained for about nine or ten months until
Wilson's wife died and she was forced to move on. For the next
two years she lived in Kettering, helping her sister there who kept
a public house. Illness – a 'gathering' in her hand – forced her into
the Northampton Infirmary for some weeks. After she was discharged by the hospital, she was supported in Northampton for

16 It is worth noting that 'the Reverend Edward Rex [sic] Free paid in £2
    8s. 0d. of the Expences incurred by Maria Crook having sworn him to
    be the father of her child now dead', WCA, St George's Hanover Square,
    Minutes of the Governors of the Poor, C 392, pp. 405, 435. I am grateful
    to David Hool for supplying me with these Westminster Archive
    references.

some time by another relative. She then went as cook to the Swan Inn at Newport Pagnell, in Buckinghamshire, where she remembered being when peace was proclaimed in 1815. Maria worked there for only about ten months, however, because the labour involved was too demanding and her health gave way. She continued to live in Newport Pagnell, maintaining herself with her needle and by working as a charwoman. At one time she diversified into making and selling sausages. In her later thirties she married George Roberts, a Newport Pagnell pedlar, but in these years she continued to maintain herself, latterly as a cap and bonnet maker. It was as the forty-three year old Maria Roberts that she testified in 1828 against Dr Free.

How Dr Free coped with his house after Maria Crook departed in 1811 we do not know. But, given her pregnancy, the prosecution launched by Bigg and the difficulties he was then having with his Oxford College,[17] it is likely that he had too much on his mind to worry immediately about such matters. His domestic and other needs were too powerful to be long resisted, however, and in the following year he recruited a successor to Maria Crook, choosing not a local woman but one then living much further afield. She was an even younger housekeeper.

Catharine Siggins was aged about eighteen, and was lodging in a court off Fleet Street in London, when at the tail end of 1812 she was hired by Dr Free and taken off to Sutton to be his housekeeper. 'Quite a young lass', as one witness later recollected, for such a position. She managed initially to resist the Rector's sexual advances, but after several months she too found herself in the clergyman's bed and became pregnant. By the summer of 1813 her condition was clearly noticeable and Free 'fearing to continue her there' arranged for her to return to London, giving her money for her confinement and delivery. There she stayed until shortly before her baby was due, at which point she returned to her father's

---

17 St John's College was pursuing him about his spoliation of the glebe. See above, Chapter 1, pp. 13–14.

house at Wade's Mill in the Hertfordshire parish of Thundridge. It was there, in the house of her fifty year old agricultural labourer father, that Dr Free's daughter was born on 21 November 1813. When after about three months the money given her by Free ran out, Catharine was obliged to turn to the parish for support. At the end of February 1814 she was examined by a magistrate and swore the child's father was Dr Free. The Rector was summoned by the magistrates to Hertford, where he agreed to recompense the parish for an allowance paid to Catharine. He also agreed to pay six shillings a week directly to the child's mother for his daughter's support. This latter sum he continued to pay as a regular quarterly payment thereafter; it was still being paid to his former housekeeper in 1828 when his daughter was aged fifteen.

Catharine continued to live with her father for about a year – 'till the said child could live without suck' – at which point she left, leaving the child behind. Nothing more of her life is known, except that at some later point she married George Raynes, a gardener of Hoxton, Middlesex. Meanwhile alarm bells were ringing back in Sutton. A Churchwarden, William Cooper, recollected in 1828 how he travelled to Hertford to get a copy of Catharine Siggins's bastardy examination from the Clerk to the Magistrates, and how this copy was presented to the Bishop of Lincoln in 1814.[18]

Catharine Siggins must have left Free's service by June 1813 because that was when he hired Margaret Johnston as her replacement.[19] She was then aged about thirty-two and was lodging in London, where she had advertised for a position. Free saw the advertisement, called on her and hired her. It was not until the autumn of that year, around the time of the birth of his daughter by Catharine Siggins, that sexual relations with Margaret Johnston began. She quickly became pregnant: a physical examination

---

18 LPL, H427/56, fol. 50r; H427/55, p. 11.
19 The following section is based largely on the testimonies of Margaret and Mary Johnston, LPL, H427/56, fos 29r–33r, 39r–40v.

obligingly conducted by an experienced neighbour, the middle-aged Mary Hale, who lived in a cottage situated close to the church yard, confirmed this.[20] As she was a thin, delicate-looking young woman, her swelling shape demanded her departure from Sutton at the end of April 1814. Where she went we do not know, but there was no shortage of establishments for women in such a predicament. The *Cambridge Chronicle and Journal* carried the following advertisement in its issue of 28 October 1809:

> Pregnant Ladies, whose situations require a temporary re-tirement, may be accommodated with apartments to Lie-in, agreeable to their circumstancess, their infants put out to nurse, and taken care of. The consolation resulting from this undertaking to many of the most respectable families in the kingdom, by securing peace and concord among relations and friends, is sufficiently conspicuous to be countenanced by the humane and sensible parts of mankind. Honour and secresy having been the basis of this concern for forty years, may be relied on; those regardless of their reputation will not be treated with. Apply to Mr or Mrs SYMONS, midwife, London House Yard, St Paul's Churchyard, London. Ladies may be accommodated in the country, if more agreeable than in town. Letters, post-paid, attended to, and advice gratis from ten to twelve.[21]

It was not in the parish of St Paul's but in the sprawling parish of Stepney, London, that Margaret gave birth to a dead female child in mid August 1814.

In September of that year she apparently returned to Dr Free's service, and to his bed, for she became pregnant again in 1816. Once more she was forced to depart the household and this time she went apparently to Ramsgate in Kent, where on 15 November she gave birth to a boy, a child who was still living when she testified at Free's trial twelve years later.

By December 1816 she was once again installed at Sutton as the

20 Ibid., fol. 99v.
21 Microfilm Collection, Central Reference Library, Cambridge.

Rector's housekeeper. Perhaps somewhat chastened and certainly wiser, sexual activity was not immediately resumed, but by the summer it had and Margaret left the Rectory again in November 1817, pregnant for the third time. This third child, another boy, was also delivered in Ramsgate, on 24 March 1818, but he subsequently died.

Margaret Johnston did not return thereafter to Sutton or to Free's employment. She certainly returned to service: by 1824 she was working for a Mr and Mrs Ricardo in London. At the time of Free's trial in the Court of Arches in 1828 she was employed as the cook-housekeeper to a Mr and Mrs William Curling of St James's Square, Westminster.

Margaret had an unmarried sister, five years older than herself, who also was called to testify at Free's trial. Mary Johnston denied knowing that her sister had ever been pregnant, though she admitted that she saw her only rarely after she had entered Dr Free's employment. She did, however, know Dr Free. Indeed the Rector had got into the habit of calling upon her in London several times a year. Nor was he her only caller. Montagu Burgoyne, hot on Free's trail, paid a surprise visit to 29 Hampden Street, Somers Town, in 1823 or 1824. Burgoyne had gone there to enquire about a child who had been placed in Mary Johnston's care by the Rector of Sutton. Whilst he was there a young boy entered the room, at which Burgoyne apparently exclaimed, 'I need not ask you whose child you are'. He went on to point out to Mary Johnston how like Dr Free the boy was, telling her in addition that he was indeed her own sister's child. Although Mary admitted guessing that Free was the boy's father, since he paid for his support and education, she denied knowing that her sister was his mother. Her story is possibly true, but it is highly improbable.

Little time elapsed between Margaret Johnston's final departure from the Rectory in November 1817 and the appointment by Dr Free of Ann Taylor as his housekeeper. Born Ann Cross, she had married a local plumber and glazier. He died, however, and she was a widow when she went into Sutton Rectory in or around

February 1818.[22] The prosecutors of Free later alleged that he several times attempted to 'take indecent liberties with her person', but that she refused to comply and she left his service at the end of 1822.[23] These allegations may have been based on information given to Montagu Burgoyne in or after 1823, when Burgoyne began to collect evidence to be used against the Rector. Ann Taylor, however, returned to Free's service in the spring of 1824 and she was still living with him in the Rectory at the time of his trial in 1828–29.[24] By that stage she was not prepared to testify against him. Free's Proctor, his attorney in the ecclesiastical court, alleged that she left in 1822 not because of 'indecent liberties' but 'in consequence of having used ... intemperate language' when remonstrated with by the Rector.[25] Ann Taylor's support is the more remarkable, given what allegedly happened in those intervening months when she was absent from Free's house.

Maria Mackenzie was a twenty-eight year old 'out-of-place' servant, living in lodgings in Somers Town, London, when, in December 1822, she responded to Dr Free's enquiries in that area and was appointed as his housekeeper.[26] Although she protested that she was a virgin at that point, about a fortnight after starting her new job she began sleeping with the Rector and this then became a nightly event. She also became pregnant, but in April 1823 she miscarried. This, she argued, was the result of an altercation with the Rector during which he knocked her down on the flagstones in a passage way in the house. Even before this, the relationship between the two had deteriorated, and Maria had announced her intention of quitting his service. Dr Free had a different story. It

22 LPL, H427/56, fos 50v, 89r.
23 These assertions are to be found in the articles or allegations that formed the basis for Free's prosecution in the Court of Arches, LPL, H427/55, p. 6.
24 LPL, H427/56, fos 70v–71r.
25 LPL, H427/20.
26 This account is based on her testimony and on her answers to the questions posed by Free to be found in LPL, H427/56, unpaginated and fos 1–15r. Free's questions are to be found in H427/37.

was that Maria was already pregnant when he hired her: the result of an affair with a man called Martin whom she had picked up in London where she was plying the trade of a common prostitute. Her miscarriage owed nothing to any action on Free's part; it was due to a venereal infection she had previously contracted, aggravated by her being kicked by a lamb that was about to be castrated. The fact of her miscarriage, however, could not be denied. She had had to remain in the Rectory for about two weeks after this mishap, and she was treated at some point by two doctors.[27]

Relationships now deteriorated further. Although there are divergent accounts of what happened, it appears that, when her period of notice to quit had elapsed, Maria had packed her boxes and demanded from the Rector the wages owing to her, a sum amounting to about £2 or £3. At this point Dr Free accused her of having taken a damask table cloth from the Rectory and also some Irish linen belonging to him. He seized her boxes and refused to pay the wages she had demanded. Maria then left and went to lodge at the home of the then Constable of Sutton, John Northfield. Although during this final confrontation at the Rectory Free threatened to call for the Constable to inspect her boxes, this threat was not carried out. The Constable did call at the Rectory, however, but, Maria maintained, it was she who had instigated it. Her story is quite remarkable. Whilst lodging with Northfield she heard a rumour that the Rector had got a new housekeeper. Such news, given their pastor's record, would have shot with great rapidity through the small community. Going past the Rectory, Maria looked up and caught sight of her own younger sister at one of the windows. In light of what she herself had suffered at the Rector's hands, Maria went immediately to fetch the Constable and together they went to the Rectory to 'claim and bring away her sister'. Free did not then make any complaint of theft to the Constable, though he repeated the charge privately to both Maria and her sister.

Before this, however, Maria, showing great spirit, had consulted

27 LPL, H427/56, fol. 4v.

a solicitor about her grievances against the Rector. What Maria would not have known was that this solicitor was that William Chapman of Biggleswade who had previously acted for Dr Free in the Bigg affair. At this point the stories once again diverge. Free maintained that it was because Chapman advised her that an action for the recovery of a sum less than £20 was only cognizable in the county court that she pursued what he alleged were trumped up charges of assault against him. Maria insisted, however, that she told Chapman the whole story at the start and that it was the attorney who advised her on her subsequent course of action. In the summer of 1823, Maria pressed charges of assault against Free at the Bedford July Quarter Sessions and the Rector was indicted to appear at a future court. Legal clerks had some difficulty in serving writs upon him because of his tendency to absent himself in order to avoid such service. The Churchwardens of Sutton complained to the Archdeacon of Bedford at the end of October that Free had absented himself since 17 August 'on account of a warrant with which the constable endeavoured to arrest him'.[28] A few days later, however, Free was bound over at the October Quarter Sessions to answer the charge of assault at the next hearings.[29]

Before this the Rector certainly visited London to brief a solicitor, Faithful Croft, to act for him. Croft appears to have advised him to settle out of court. Early in August Maria apparently agreed to halt proceedings against Free in return for the payment of ten guineas and all the legal expenses she had incurred. Difficulties subsequently ensued over these costs, however, because William Chapman entered a claim for more than £17 and the Rector refused to pay up. Faithful Croft apparently exclaimed that he, Croft, would

28 LPL, H427/55, p. 11.
29 BRO, QSR 1823/230a is a recognizance, dated 28 October 1823, entered into by Dr Free 'now of No. 44 Speldhurst Street, Burton Crescent, in the county of Middlesex', John Corbett, linguist, of the same address, and Charles North Hunt, gentleman, of 6 Hadlow Street, Middlesex, for Free to appear at the next Sessions of the Peace for the county of Bedford to answer an 'Indictment against him for assaulting one Mary Mackenzie Spinster'.

have done twice the business for the same money. As a consequence, and perhaps at Chapman's instigation, Maria's prosecution of Free for assault went ahead.[30]

At the Bedford February Sessions, however, events took a further and unexpected turn, for a Mr Budd, an attorney who it subsequently transpired was acting for Montagu Burgoyne, interfered and opposed the application from Free's attorney for the indictment against him to be quashed. Bail was then apparently given to Dr Free, and the cause was subsequently removed to King's Bench, seemingly on the grounds that Free was incapable of getting a fair hearing in Bedford because of local hostility to him. According to Free, the Attorney General, after hearing solicitors on both sides, granted a *nolle prosequi* (a ruling that the case should not proceed) on payment by the Rector of Chapman's costs and Maria's backwages of £3.[31] According to her testimony, however, these wages were never recovered from the Rector.

30   LPL, H427/56, Maria Mackenzie's deposition, no folio.
31   Between 26 June and 6 July 1824 three affidavits were entered at the King's Bench. The first of these, from Dr Free, stated that at the Bedford Quarter Sessions held on 16 July 1823 he faced an indictment for assaulting Maria Mackenzie, and to avoid possible degradation of his reputation he subsequently authorised his solicitor to settle with her out of court. Maria was paid ten guineas and thereupon executed a 'general release' against Free. Nevertheless, the prosecution was continuing, provoked by the ill will borne by the inhabitants of Sutton against him, and particularly that of Montagu Burgoyne, so that it was impossible for him to have a fair trial in the county of Bedford. Maria's affidavit, of 3 July, emphasised Free's guilt in relation to the charges pressed upon him, but explained that she became apprehensive about Chapman's mounting legal charges and, fearing that she might be sent to prison if she failed to meet his bill of more than £17, she was persuaded by Free's solicitor to sign the release against him. He agreed to pay her ten guineas and also to pay Chapman's bill. But the Rector subsequently demurred in relation to the latter, causing her to regret the whole arrangement. It was for this reason and also 'her Duty to the Public' that the prosecution was continuing. She pointed out, moreover, that the witnesses she hoped to call all resided in or about Potton, making it impossible for her to continue her prosecution if a venue for the trial other than Bedford was chosen. The last affidavit came from Burgoyne. He denied bearing

Maria Mackenzie's subsequent history has something in common with Maria Crook's, revealing much about the precarious nature of domestic service and the resourcefulness of female servants in the face of difficulties and uncertainties. After leaving the Rectory she lodged for about a month in John Northfield's house in Sutton. She then returned to her mother's house in Somers Town, London, staying there to recover from her illness. When she had regained her strength, she found a place in the household of a Mr Walker, near the Elephant and Castle. All she could recollect of this situation years later when testifying was that Mr Walker had something to do with the 'Mendicity Society'. After about two months she left this place for service with an organ-builder called Mayers who lived by Old Pancras Church. There she stayed for three months before returning to her mother's house, maintaining herself whilst out of work by selling some of her clothing. Next she went into the service of Messrs Bury and Reed, at the corner of King Street, Holborn, where she remained for two years.

Whilst in the summer of 1823 he was being pursued through the courts by Maria Mackenzie, Dr Free engaged yet another housekeeper. This was the twenty-eight year old Mary Pierson, who preferred to be called Eliza Pierson. Described by one witness as 'a smart dressy young woman', she had advertised in a newspaper for a position. Dr Free offered her the post of his housekeeper, backed up it seems by some reassuring references that he also provided. On the strength of this Eliza travelled to Sutton in June 1823 to take up her new post. She left after about nine days, however, repelled by Dr Free's sexual overtures. So unwelcome were these advances that Eliza quitted his service without giving

---

personal ill will towards Free, and professed that his interest was 'to prevent public Justice from being defeated and to protect Maria Mackenzie' from being 'grossly injured by the said Edward Drax Free and extremely ill treated by the Attorney': Public Record Office [hereafter PRO], KB 1/46, part 5, no. 42; part 6, no. 89.

notice, lodging for a while with a widow in a cottage in Sutton before returning to London.

The whole was an extraordinary sequence of events. Free's known procreative career began rather late in life. He was nearly forty-four when he arrived in Sutton, and forty-six when he fathered Maria Crook's baby. He was forty-nine when Catharine Siggins' child was born, and between the ages of fifty and fifty-four he fathered three more illegitimate children by Margaret Johnston. Ann Taylor was a widow when she became Free's housekeeper, and perhaps past childbearing. The Rector was clearly still sexually active, however, because he managed at the age of fifty-eight to get Maria Mackenzie pregnant, though she subsequently miscarried. Being pursued at law by Maria did not stop him from attempting to seduce Eliza Pierson.

All these women, with the possible exception of Ann Taylor, were much younger than he was. Maria Crook was twenty-five when she first went to work in the Rectory; Catharine Siggins was a mere eighteen; Margaret Johnston was about thirty-two, four years older than Maria Mackenzie, who at twenty-eight was the same age as Eliza Pierson.

The Rector was, however, far from being the middle-aged gallant who irresistibly drew a succession of young women into his bed. The testimonies of these housekeepers shed some light on his methods of seduction: they were clearly subjected to a considerable amount of sexual harassment.

One complaint was that they were obliged to live alone with the Rector; there were no other live-in servants. What is more, the Rectory was shut up in the evening and visitors were turned away. Margaret Johnston deposed that Free 'never went out after dark, and never suffered his gate to be opened after dark, ring at it who would'.[32] Eliza Pierson declared also that she was uneasy about 'the House being shut up at an early hour every Evening'

32 LPL, H427/56, fol. 33r.

for 'she felt that she should have difficulty in making herself heard'.[33] It was then that the Rector began to drink his favourite tipple of rum and water.[34]

Eliza Pierson also expressed disquiet about her sleeping quarters. On the night of her arrival the Rector showed her to her bedroom. This, she discovered, was right next to his bedroom, and the two rooms were interconnected by a door. Dr Free, she deposed, 'would have that door kept open, and she had no means of fastening it'. So disquieted was she that she moved her bed to another part of the house, much to the Rector's displeasure. One night, during her brief stay in the house, she was roused by Dr Free vigorously ringing his bell, so vigorously in fact that Eliza feared he was ill, perhaps even dying. But, as she later related, 'from his manner in asking her to come to him in bed', she realised he was far from being ill, made her excuses and returned to her own room.[35] Maria Mackenzie deposed that during the daytime she had answered the parlour bell and found the Rector stripped naked below the waist.[36] Eliza Pierson only ever saw the upper reaches of the Rector: not apparently a pretty sight. 'He used to go about the House during a great part of the Day in his Dressing Gown', she related, 'which he used to throw open so as to show his bosom', an area disfigured with some sort of skin infection.[37]

His person was not the only thing he showed these young women. Maria Mackenzie remembered being shown a book of prints – 'very bad, very indecent and obscene'. She could not bring herself to look at them: 'they were too bad, and too bad to be described'.[38] Maria Crook, on the other hand, had no recollection of being shown any obscene books, but she recalled of the Rector that 'his Conversation was very unbecoming at times, and very indecent'.[39]

33 Ibid., fol. 43v.
34 Ibid., fol. 29v.
35 Ibid., fos 43r and v.
36 Ibid., no folio.
37 Ibid., fol. 44r.
38 Ibid., no folio.
39 Ibid., fol. 35v.

The books certainly existed. Free's handyman James Steers remembered finding one in the sitting room on a table alongside the chair in which the Rector usually sat. Curiosity got the better of him. It was apparently a copy of *Aristotle's Masterpiece*, perhaps the earliest English sex manual. Steers did not read any of the text, but he looked at the illustrations: 'They represented naked Men and Women in carnal connexion with each other; in different situations, standing, lying, sitting; all of the most indecent kind.'[40] Eliza Pierson could not recall seeing any such literature, but she complained about the way in which the Rector used to follow her around the house, attempting to kiss her whilst boasting about his amours.[41]

Although Eliza Pierson stayed on in the village for no more than two weeks, it was long enough for her to make the acquaintance of Maria Mackenzie and for the two young women to swap stories of their experiences at the Rectory. They clearly had more than their ages in common. Dr Free must have been alarmed by this development because he attempted to force Eliza Pierson out of the village, telling the widow who was housing her that the young woman had robbed him and that she should put her out. Eliza, alerted no doubt by Maria to the character of the man she was dealing with, supposedly said to the Rector, 'You have said that of others; if you dare repeat it of me, if there is law or justice to be had I'll punish you'.

The autumn of 1823 saw the process of retribution beginning: Dr Free was the subject of a series of complaints, organised by Montagu Burgoyne, and rendered in formal presentments made by the Churchwardens and others to the Archdeacon of Bedford. By this time Free was widely loathed in Sutton. The hatred felt for him was not entirely the result of his sexual misconduct; it owed more to the way in which he performed his clerical duties and to the ways in which he conducted himself in his day to day dealings with his parishioners. To these aspects we must now turn.

40 Ibid., fol. 69v.
41 Ibid., fol. 43v.

3

The Parish Priest

A NGLICANISM was, in several senses, a broad church. With over
10,000 parishes in England and, despite pluralism, perhaps as
many clergymen, it offered career openings to substantial numbers
each year. The securing of a parish living depended not on one's
personal qualities but on one's access to, and relationship with, a
patron with rights of presentation to such livings. An extraordinarily
wide range of characters consequently found themselves installed
in country parishes. They included saints and sinners, the idle and
industrious, the sane and the eccentric, the genuinely devout and
those content merely to go through the motions of devotion.
Parishioners had learned as a result to tolerate all sorts of personal
idiosyncrasies in their clergymen, but they also had expectations of
them.[1]

What did villagers expect of their cleric? They expected that 'the
duty' – divine service – would be conducted at prescribed times,
and in a dignified manner. They expected that their pastor would
perform the rites appropriate to baptism, churching, marriage and
death, as and when they were required. These were perhaps minimal
expectations; anything beyond this was a welcome bonus. A clergyman might be expected also to visit the sick and the aged, to be
generous to the respectable poor, and to involve himself in charitable

---

1 Irene Collins, *Jane Austen and the Clergy* (London, 1994), supplies an
   admirable introduction to the world of the country clergyman at the
   time of Dr Free. Jane Austen's brothers, James and Henry, both went
   up to St John's where they were contemporaries of Dr Free.

works in the community. This benevolence should also stretch to those who were his tenants and those who worked for him. He should not take advantage of people who were dependent upon him, but should behave towards them in a proper Christian manner. Finally, villagers expected the fabric of their church to be maintained. Whilst this was legally the responsibility of the vestry, with the Rector being responsible legally for the chancel, in practice the responsibilities of oversight and care must have been shared by both the incumbent and the vestry. Villagers certainly did not expect their pastor to pillage the church. The same expectations applied to the churchyard, where their kin and friends were buried. Dr Free fell sadly short in relation to each and every one of these expectations.[2]

Our knowledge of his failings is derived largely, but not entirely, from the complaints that were made by parishioners deposing in his trial in the Court of Arches in the later 1820s; and by then their bitterness had probably grown in compound fashion. Similarly the picture that they presented of his predecessor, Dr Kettilby, may also be coloured, but in reverse fashion: almost any pastor would

---

2 Splendid accounts of two highly eccentric clergymen – John Skinner (1772–1839) and Robert Stephen Hawker (1803–75) – are to be found in H. and P. Coombs, *Journal of a Somerset Rector* (Oxford, 1984), and P. Brendon, *Hawker of Morwenstow* (London, 1975). Dr Brendon draws attention to 'J. A. Froude's admirably generalised portrait of the "average incumbent" of the 1830s ... Froude, himself the son of a West Country clergyman, described the typical parson as a man of private fortune ... His professional duties were his services on Sunday, funerals and weddings on week-days, and visits when needed among the sick. In other respects he lived like his neighbours ... He farmed his own glebe; he kept horses ... he attended public meetings, and his education enabled him to take a leading part in country business. His wife and daughters looked after the poor, taught in the Sunday school, and managed the penny clubs and clothing clubs. He himself was spoken of in the parish as "the master" – the person who was responsible for keeping order there, and who knew how to keep it. The labourers and the farmers looked up to him. The "family" in the great house could hardly look down upon him', ibid., pp. 81–82. If this represented an ideal type, then, as we shall see, Dr Free clearly failed to match it.

4. Thomas Fisher's sketch of All Saints, Sutton, *c.* 1810
(*Bedfordshire Record Office*)

have been remembered as a saint by comparison with Edward Drax
Free.

Few in Sutton had longer memories than Robert Oake, who
was aged eighty when he made his deposition in December 1828.
He was not alone in recalling that the church used to be well

attended on a Sunday before Dr Free arrived: 'The farmers came to church in Dr Kettilby's time, and as the great house was up then, and the family lived in it, they came too.'[3] Mary Hale, a seventy-six year old widow, supported this story: 'Farmers as well as the poor attended then, and the family at the great house, the Park, which is down now ...'[4] So also did John Northfield, a former Parish Clerk and Constable: 'During Doctor Kettilby's incumbency a fair proportion of the parishioners, farmers as well as the labourers and the family from the Park, used to attend the church.'[5]

No doubt many new faces showed up when Dr Free first arrived, curious to see and hear their new minister. Robert Oake attested that 'Dr Free had a good congregation at first: but it did not last long', and John Northfield said of the numbers attending, 'They soon fell off after Doctor Free came'.[6] The sixty year old William Cooper, farmer and former Churchwarden, was another who remembered the transition between incumbents:

> In the time of Dr Kettilby ... divine service was performed in the parish church at Sutton very regularly; always once and as the deponent now recollects more commonly twice every Sunday.[7] Doctor Free, for some time after he came, used to perform the service regularly: the morning service with a sermon. To the particular Sundays on which the duty has been omitted, the deponent cannot from recollection depose. It was omitted, and as he believes neglected, at one period for several weeks together ... The deponent knows of no reason, besides the absence of Dr Free, for the omission of divine service in the church of Sutton.[8]

3 LPL, H427/56, fol. 111v. Sutton Park burnt down in 1825.
4 Ibid., fol. 102r.
5 Ibid., fol. 80v.
6 Ibid., fos 80v, 111v.
7 William Hale deposed that 'there was service in the church of Sutton regularly; twice every Sunday when Doctor Kettilby was there, and once when he was away', ibid., fol. 16v.
8 Ibid., fol. 51r.

Others shared these memories. During the prosecution that Free inadvisedly brought against Sir Montagu Burgoyne in 1817 for failing to attend church, the Churchwardens brought out the fact that Sutton church was closed for lengthy periods in 1815,[9] and in the Court of Arches case in 1828 Free was also charged with failing to provide services between 25 November and 24 December 1820, and on other days in 1819 and 1821.[10] John Bowyer, another former Churchwarden, thought that services were neglected in these years for as many as fifteen or sixteen weeks.[11] The presentments made to the Archdeacon of Bedford in October 1823 stated that Free had been absent from his church since the previous August 'on account of a warrant with which the Constable endeavoured to arrest him'. It was then, of course, that the Rector was facing charges of having assaulted Maria Mackenzie. In 1829 he was also confined for a time in the King's Bench prison for debt. This was for failing to pay Faithful Croft the great bulk of the £968 of legal expenses that the Rector owed his attorney.[12] Montagu Burgoyne, who reported his incarceration to the Bishop of Lincoln, was asked, as Churchwarden, 'to provide for the duty at Sutton'.[13]

The prosecution of Burgoyne in 1817 also provided opportunities for the defence counsel to complain that 'the reverend plaintiff was so inattentive to the performance of the religious service of his church, that his parishioners were constantly in a state of uncertainty as to the hour at which the service was to commence, or whether it would be performed at all'.[14] William Hale deposed in 1828 that 'Since he has been there sometimes the bell has tolled out but there was no service, and at other times there was no bell and no service'.[15]

---

9 See Chapter 4.

10 LPL, H427/55, p. 7, and Article 17 of Appendix 4 below, pp. 160–61.

11 LPL, H427/56, fol. 124r.

12 PRO, King's Bench Prison Commitment Book, PRIS 4/40, p. 167.

13 St John's College, MS L10 (vii); Burgoyne, *A Letter from Montagu Burgoyne Esq., Churchwarden of Sutton, to his Brother Churchwardens in the Diocese of Lincoln* (London, 1830), p. 6.

14 *Annual Register for the Year 1817* (London, 1818), p. 195.

15 LPL, H427/56, fol. 16v.

When something like regularity prevailed, Dr Free seems to have aimed at providing Sunday services in the morning one week, followed by an afternoon service on the following Sunday. The Rector, however, was frequently not at his best in the mornings. One witness noticed how 'Doctor Free was in the morning nervous and shaky, and continued so till after his dinner, when he seemed to recover his spirits', a condition the witness attributed to the Rector's drinking habits.[16]

There were a few who had no complaints about the manner in which the rituals were conducted. A labourer's wife, Amy Randall, attested that 'The church service had always been performed ...', when she attended, 'with great decency and propriety'; and Phoebe Smith, a widow, admitted that 'he can do the duty well if he will'.[17] But there were very many more who complained of the ways in which Free conducted himself in church. 'Doctor Free can do the service, prayers and preaching well if he is minded, as most can and better than many', Robert Oake attested, 'and he can do it as ill, and does oftentimes.'[18] William Coxall, a farmer and former Churchwarden, wrote that when he

> had heard Doctor Free do the duty there has been that sort of manner with him which was offensive to the respondent, an indifference about him; lounging on one side and the other, not like a man who was in earnest or wished others to be in earnest; but as if he said, I do it because I must do it; I had rather not be troubled with it, and the sooner it is done the better ...[19]

Services were certainly performed hastily. 'He goes through it pretty quickly sometimes', said William Dazeley, and Robert Oake deposed that if Free was in that sort of mood, 'He will do the whole in about half the time that is usual'.[20]

16 Ibid., fol. 69v.
17 Ibid., fos 105r, 116r.
18 Ibid., fol. 111r.
19 Ibid., fol. 65v.
20 Ibid., fos 97r, 111r.

The congregation did not always get a sermon and when one was provided it often turned into a diatribe against those whom he thought were persecuting him. William Dazeley did not see why the Rector 'should introduce his law business in his sermons', whilst Phoebe Smith complained not only that 'They have been in and out again within the half hour many times', but also that 'What Doctor Free says in the pulpit is more about his enemies and those who have offended him than anything else'.[21]

Some of the most serious complaints were those directed at his failure to perform the rites associated with birth and death. One Saturday evening in October 1820 the three year old son of John and Mary Saville, 'a very fine fat child', died after a sudden illness. On the following Monday the parents sent word to the Rector that they would like the child to be buried the next day, the Tuesday. Unfortunately the woman who carried the message for the distraught parents had the temerity to speak to Dr Free in the street, and was roundly scolded as an 'impertinent woman' for doing so. Later that Monday the corpse began to both swell and smell, bursting the coffin on the Tuesday, the day they had hoped that the burial might take place, and creating a problem in their dwelling, 'pinched for room as they were'. The child was not in fact interred by Free until the Wednesday, despite a plea on the Tuesday morning from Robert Oake, Mary Saville's father, that the corpse was not fit to be kept any longer and should be buried that Tuesday afternoon, the grave having already been dug.[22]

Thomas and Phoebe Smith, who suffered the death of one of their children in May 1823, experienced a distinct lack of charity and sympathy at the hands of the Rector. At the time arranged for the burial they took the body to the churchyard gate. There they were met by the Clerk who demanded four shillings from them. Phoebe Smith had anticipated this, and the money had indeed been handed over to her by the Overseer of the Poor. She forgot to

21 Ibid., fos 97r, 116r.
22 Ibid., fos 109r, 132r and v.

bring it with her, however, and it was still in the tea-chest where she had placed it for safety. Thomas Smith was apparently summoned into the Rectory, and when he came back twenty minutes later he wanted to go home to fetch the money. Phoebe demurred, however, insisting that the burial should take place first. The Rector eventually came out and performed the burial service, though the Clerk followed them home to collect the fee.[23]

Another labourer, also called Thomas Smith, related in 1828 how one Sunday afternoon in January 1821 he and his wife, since dead, went to the church accompanied by a godfather and two godmothers to get their month-old daughter baptised. Briefed by Dr Free, the Parish Clerk demanded a fee of eighteen pence for christening the baby and churching the wife. After this was handed over, the Rector apparently claimed that this was not payment for the services they then expected to receive: it was payment still owing from a previous birth – and he demanded eighteen pence more. Thomas Smith refused to pay any more, claiming that the Rector still owed him double that amount for work he had undertaken for him. They had 'a good deal of cavil more' in the church, with Free refusing eventually to baptise the child or church the wife until the fee was paid. The child never was baptised, and presumably the wife never churched.

Amy Randall, the wife of a labourer of Sutton, testified that she went to church one Sunday in August 1823, with her husband and new-born child, for the dual ceremony of churching and christening, but the Rector left the pulpit without performing either ceremony. When she went after him, he told her to come the next Sunday. This she did, but once again Free left the pulpit, saying to her that he would not baptise the child without her paying a fee of a shilling. This, she explained, she did not have. The Rector responded by saying that she should have asked the Overseer for it, but Amy argued that even if she had done this he would not have given it to her. A little while later, Free apparently relented

---

23   Ibid., fol. 114v.

and baptised their child, saying that as she was a poor woman he would baptise it without a fee. When the ceremony was over, however, Dr Free requested that James Randall, Amy's husband, step forward. When James did so, Free demanded to know who employed him and how much he received in harvest wages. When he replied that he was employed by John Bowyer, a local farmer, and that his harvest wage was forty-five shillings, Dr Free allegedly said, 'Can't you spare a shilling out of that for Christening your child?' Randall said that he had not got a shilling on him but that he would bring one next Sunday. This provoked his wife, Amy, who said that he should do no such thing, since the Rector had offered to christen it for nothing. At that point Free exploded and ordered her out of the church.[24]

William Coxall, one of the larger farmers in the community, took his wife to Sutton church one Sunday in 1826 for her to be churched, a ceremony that was usually performed after divine service. She emerged from the church, however, without it having been performed. Coxall, who had sat outside in the porch, claiming that he was late for the service because he had had to tie up his horse and carriage, went into the church and requested that the Rector should church his wife. Free, outraged by Coxall's absence, ordered him from the building, threatening to call upon the Clerk to eject him physically if he did not do so. Coxall then made formal application through the Clerk for his wife to be churched on a weekday. This the Rector refused to do.[25]

Another of Sutton's farmers, John Bowyer, had several disputes with the Rector, with at least one of them verging on physical violence. In 1827 Bowyer's brother, who was then dying, obtained from Free a promise that he could be buried alongside his father in Sutton churchyard, despite his not being resident in the village. At the very last moment, when preparations for Thomas Bowyer's

---

24 Ibid., fos 83r, 104r. LPL, H427/48, makes it clear that these events were spread over two Sundays.
25 LPL, H427/56, fos 67r and v.

funeral had all been made, the Rector changed his mind, refusing to allow the burial to take place unless John Bowyer paid a fee of £2 7s. 0d., and a further pound in settlement of a dispute between the two of them over a crop of potatoes. The incident bears out William Cooper's complaint of Free that he quarrelled with all and sundry, and that 'he cannot perform a funeral without wrangling with someone'.[26]

The dispute about potatoes went back to 1826 when Dr Free claimed that Bowyer's hogs had broken into the Rectory close and had eaten up a crop of potatoes growing in his orchard.[27] He claimed a pound in damages from the farmer. Bowyer did not deny that his pigs had a propensity to trespass, but blamed it on the Rector's unwillingness to maintain the fence between their neighbouring properties, as he was legally obliged to. An estimator was apparently brought in and, according to Bowyer, he found that not only was no damage done but also there were no potatoes growing there at that time.[28]

This duplicity seems to have been typical of Dr Free. James Steers once worked as the Rector's handyman and had experience of it. Steers thought that it was not becoming for a clergyman 'to cheat poor people of their money, as he did in many instances, picking quarrels with them, abusing them, and turning them away without paying them'. Steers worked for Free for less than a year, leaving in May 1823 after several disputes, the last of them about a bank errand. Steers was sent to London by Free in October 1822 with orders to cash a cheque for £10 at Child's Bank. On his return he handed over only £5. Free claimed subsequently that Steers had pocketed the remainder, and that the handyman had told the housekeeper that he had been set upon and robbed on the way. Steers denied telling Ann Taylor any such story, claiming that he retained the other £5, with Free's consent, for wages owing to

26 Ibid., fol. 56v.
27 LPL, H427/44.
28 LPL, H427/56, fos 131r and v.

him. He also deposed that, on leaving Free's service, he was obliged to sue for the balance of his wages. This bears out William Coxall's statement that 'Warrants have been out against him repeatedly for not paying those who have worked for him', and perhaps William Dazeley's remark that 'He will resort to any trick to defraud people'.[29]

Shopkeepers also suffered at the Rector's hands. William Bigg, a Potton shopkeeper, went to the Rectory at Sutton in the early evening of Friday 7 December 1810 in order to present Dr Free with a small, but no doubt overdue, bill. He was shown by Maria Crook into the parlour where the Rector and the Reverend Edward Mossop, Vicar of Langford, were sat each side of the fire drinking wine.[30] Bigg presented his bill, which the Rector then denied was owing. Calling Bigg 'Villain, rascal, scoundrel, cheat, Methodist', he seized the shopkeeper by an arm and his coat collar and forced him from the room. Not content with this he grabbed hold of Dr Mossop's stick and threatened to cudgel Bigg unless he immediately left the house. Pushing him down the long passageway to the wash-house, he flung him out of the door.[31] Bigg lost little time in complaining to Samuel Whitbread, the Biggleswade magistrate, who wrote to Dr Free 'advising him to compromise the matter'.[32] Free felt sufficiently alarmed by his own behaviour to approach a local solicitor, William Chapman of Biggleswade, who interceded with Whitbread on Free's behalf. 'Dr Free', he wrote to the magistrate, 'being so well satisfied of the propriety of his conduct towards Biggs [sic], and having such respectable evidence in confirmation of it, begs me to say he does not conceive that he has

29 Ibid., fos 65v, 72r–74r, 96r.
30 George Edward Mossop, Vicar of Langford, Bedfordshire, a Cumbrian and graduate of St John's, Cambridge: see *Admission to the College of St John the Evangelist in the University of Cambridge*, ed. R. F. Scott, iv (Cambridge, 1931), p. 391.
31 This is the story recounted by William Bigg on 7 January 1811 in the complaint laid before James Webster, JP. See BRO, QSR 1811/139.
32 *Samuel Whitbread's Notebooks, 1810–11, 1813–14*, ed. A. F. Cirket (Bedford, 1971), p. 30.

any matter whatever to accommodate with Biggs.' Free also wrote directly to Whitbread, pleading that his health prohibited early and long rides, unless absolutely necessary, and expressing the hope that Mossop's evidence would see him clear.[33]

Events duly took their course. Whitbread's notebook records that on Boxing Day Bigg and the Constable of Sutton came to see him, the latter reporting that, when he had tried to serve a warrant on Free at eight o'clock that morning he had been told by a servant that the Rector had departed for London the previous evening by the mail coach. The Constable was ordered to conduct a search to confirm the truth of this allegation and, if true, to execute his warrant on the clergyman's return. On 10 January 1811 Free, Bigg, Mossop, Maria Crook and a former servant of the Rector's, John Hipwell, appeared before another Justice of the Peace, James Webster of Meppershall, who bound the protagonists to appear at the next Bedford Quarter Sessions. Webster was clearly swayed by Bigg's story, and not at all persuaded by the support for the Rector that came from Mossop – 'a great friend and table companion of the Doctor's'. He also resisted Dr Free's threat that he would consult London counsel, and his plea that the case should go to the Assizes.[34] Eventually, at Quarter Sessions, the jurors found Free guilty of assaulting Bigg, and the Rector was fined £5.[35]

It was not this incident that lay behind the accusation in the presentments made to the Archdeacon of Bedford thirteen years later, when the Rector was charged with being 'guilty of swindling and shoplifting'. It was William Cooper who then accused him of shoplifting 'on the authority of an ironmonger of Biggleswade', and as for swindling this Cooper could detail 'from his own knowledge and experience in many instances'.[36]

Free claimed that he had 'at all times shown himself ready to

33 BRO, W1 316–17.
34 BRO, W1 319.
35 BRO, QSR 1811/269; *Samuel Whitbread's Notebooks*, ed. Cirket, pp. 31–32.
36 LPL, H427/55, p. 11; H427/56, fol. 55v.

attend the sick and poor, and [he] has not only relieved them various ways but restored their health in various cases where they have followed his advice'.[37] Only a very few, however, put in a good word for him. Jane Northfield said that 'he behaved kindly to her in allowing her still-born child to be laid in a grave', but she also voiced complaints about the state of the graveyard.[38] More were prepared to insist, like William Cooper, that 'he never goes to see a sick person in the parish', though Cooper also doubted 'whether there was one person in the parish who would allow him to enter the house'.[39] John Bowyer also complained that Free 'never attends the poor or visits the sick'. He was forever quarrelling: 'an insane man', he called him.[40]

His fuse was certainly notoriously short, and those who worked for him suffered much abuse. James Steers thought he was behaving wisely when he put one of a pair of lambs to a ewe that had just lost her own. The lamb unfortunately died, but when Free discovered what had happened he exploded, calling Steers all 'the names he could put his tongue to' and 'went on in that way till he was tired'. Steers then went off to milk the Rector's cow, eventually calling at the Rectory for a customary half pint of beer. This provoked the Rector into a fresh round of abuse. 'He was like a madman for rage at the time', deposed poor James Steers.[41]

One with early experience of Free's ill temper was William Tear of Potton, a young bricklayer employed by Free to repair the Rectory soon after he took up his living. Tear was later employed by the parish and he recounted how the Rector would come up to him repeatedly while he was at work at the church 'doing parish work', and would abuse him shamefully, threatening him with a stick, and behaving in such a way as to make him think that the Rector must have been under the influence of drink. On another

37 LPL, H427/48.
38 LPL, H427/56, fol. 91v.
39 Ibid., fol. 56v.
40 Ibid., 128v.
41 Ibid., fol. 70r.

occasion Tear was employed in laying a drain in the churchyard, a drain that had been advised by a surveyor, alerted it was said by the Archdeacon, concerned about the fabric of the church.[42] Tear was being directed, however, by Montagu Burgoyne, and it was almost certainly this that provoked the Rector into another of his rages, an event that led to Free confiscating Tear's tools and Tear threatening the cleric. The episode culminated in John Northfield, the Constable, standing by to keep the peace whilst the work was completed.[43]

The Rector seems to have been almost continuously at war with the vestry. A lot of trouble revolved around keys and consequently around access to the church. Several senior residents swore that there always used to be two keys to the main door of the church, one of which was retained by the Rector, the other by the Churchwarden. At some point Dr Free obtained possession of the second key and, in characteristic fashion, refused to relinquish it. He was also the sole possessor of the key to the chancel door. Apparently he objected to the vestry holding their annual meeting on any day other than Easter Monday, whilst they preferred to meet on a Thursday. When the vestry called their meetings and assembled at the church they could not gain access. John Bowyer, frustrated by this, had a duplicate key specially made. Free retaliated by fixing a bolt to the inside of the porch door so that they still could not gain access. In 1821, 1823 and 1824, Bowyer deposed, the parishioners were prevented from so entering their church.[44] The war went on thereafter. The vestry minute book records in 1825 that 'At a Vestry holden this 26th day of March, in the church-porch, the minister having refused to open the church doors, and adjourned to Mr Bowyer's Brook Farm, a Rate of one shilling

---

42 The Vestry Minutes record, 9 August 1824, that 'Mr Montagu Burgoyne informed the meeting that he had found it his duty to order the Church to be put into proper repair according to the directions of the Archdeacon and the opinion of Mr Swepson, an eminent surveyor of Bedford ...', BRO, P123/5/1, no pagination.

43 LPL, H427/56, fol. 88r.

44 Ibid., fol. 125r.

I. The Merchant Taylors' school-room (*Cambridge University Library*)

II. St John's College, Oxford (*Cambridge University Library*)

III. Sutton Rectory in late Victorian times (*Ann Brady*)

IV. The half-timbered wing of Sutton Rectory, with the church beyond
(*R.B. Outhwaite*)

V. All Saints, Sutton (*R.B. Outhwaite*)

VI. The pulpit, All Saints, Sutton, from which Dr Free
harangued his enemies (*R.B.Outhwaite*)

VII. The loft, All Saints, Sutton, where Dr Free allegedly kept pigeons, and the organ, later installed by Montagu Burgoyne (*R.B.Outhwaite*)

VIII. Burgoyne monuments, All Saints, Sutton (*R.B.Outhwaite*)

IX. The King's Bench prison (*Cambridge University Library*)

X. Doctors' Commons (*Cambridge University Library*)

XI. The Court of King's Bench (*Cambridge University Library*)

XII. The church porch, All Saints, Sutton, where Dr Free foddered his livestock, with the Rectory behind (*R.B.Outhwaite*)

was granted to the Church-Wardens'.[45] This provoked Montagu Burgoyne, who had become Churchwarden of Sutton, to present a series of complaints a week later to the Archdeacon at Bedford. Not only had Free refused the vestry the use of the church, forcing those attending to hold their meeting in the porch, he also refused them access to the church to examine repairs or to regulate the clock. Dr Free makes the clock, complained Burgoyne, 'go faster or slower according to his convenience'. Not only this, but he was keeping pigeons in the church belfry, where nests had been fitted up for them. The Rector was also accused of retaining in his own possession certain parochial trust deeds and of refusing to deliver copies of the parish register. The most serious charge was that on Sunday 3 April, Easter Day, he was 'guilty of brawling in the church during divine service, loudly scolding the Clerk for giving notice of a vestry by desire of the churchwarden and parishioners called for Thursday in Easter week for the purpose of electing church-wardens'.[46]

The farmers were no doubt well represented in the Sutton vestry, and the Rector's relationship with that body would not have been helped by the fact that he had quarrelled with many of his nine farming neighbours. One such was Thomas Brown, who farmed some grassland that was tithable when it was tilled. A year after Free's arrival Brown grew a crop of turnips on about eight acres of this land. According to the farmer, he and the Rector viewed the crop, agreed it was bad, and fixed a sum for the tithe. Then, whilst the Rector was away, the farmer turned his sheep upon the crop. On his return, Dr Free refused to stand by the valuation formerly agreed and made Brown pay 'more than the whole crop was worth'. The farmer took legal advice but his attorney advised settlement rather than going to law. In the following year, 1810–11, when Brown grew corn on the land, Free claimed tithe on it. The farmer then let the land return to grass.[47]

45 BRO, P123/5/1.
46 BRO, ABC/17; ABCP 391/12; ABCV 89.
47 LPL, H427/56, fos 119v, 122v–123r.

John Bowyer not only had the dispute of 1826 over his pigs allegedly consuming Free's potatoes, there was also a major confrontation before this over a lock on the churchyard gate. The Rector apparently kept the churchyard locked. Bowyer, who was Churchwarden at the time, climbed, along with James Papworth, a carpenter, over the yard wall, broke off the old lock and put on a new one. Two new keys were made: one was sent to Free; the other Bowyer kept. This led to a confrontation between the two of them, with Bowyer claiming that Free raised a hammer against him, threatening to smash open his skull.[48]

William Coxall worked about 400 acres, one of the largest farms in the village. Some of his mother's livestock twice got into a meadow belonging to their clerical neighbour, destroying and eating his hay, or so the Rector claimed. This was entirely the result, Coxall counter-claimed, of the Rector neglecting his fences, despite constant entreaties not to do so and the erection of hurdles and other barriers by Coxall on his side of the boundary. A brook constituted the boundary in one place and, to stop his cattle wandering into the stream and then crossing over into his neighbour's land, Coxall had constructed a fence of posts and rails across the flow. The Rector insisted, however, that the boundary ran down the middle of the stream, and pulled down the fence, thus allowing the cattle to intrude.[49]

William Cooper had many battles with the Rector and he was Churchwarden at the time that serious complaints were made to the Archdeacon in 1823. His signature headed the list of those who signed these complaints. Amongst the other seven signatories of these presentments are to be found the names of William Coxall, John Bowyer and Thomas Brown.[50]

Almost from the time of his arrival Dr Free seems to have antagonised his farming neighbours. In his predecessor's time part

48 Ibid., fol. 131r. Free claimed, however, that it was Bowyer who threatened him with a hammer, H427/44.
49 LPL, H427/44; H427/56, fol. 67r.
50 LPL, H427/55, pp. 11–12.

of the glebe land belonging to the Rector had been let to a Mr Green. William Coxall's father also farmed about seventeen acres of it, and a Mr Saunderson about ten acres. Coxall's father paid a rent of about two pounds or two guineas an acre. One of Free's first actions was to take it back into his own hands, then to let it at such enhanced rents that sometimes his tenants were unable to pay. At least one 'broke' and was distrained on by his clerical landlord. John Bowyer testified in 1828 that Free's unwillingness to let the glebe at a fair rent meant that he had to retain it in his own hands and 'from the state and condition of it, he can have made very little by it'.[51] There appears to be some truth in the assertion that Free attempted to rack-rent the glebe. Writing to St John's College in 1821, he claimed that whereas Dr Kettilby had let twenty-seven acres of glebe for £32 5s. od., he was charging £105 for the same.[52]

The Rector argued also that there had been encroachments on the glebe. He claimed possession of a lane bounding his property, throwing down an intervening fence in the process, and he claimed also a neighbouring willow row. These acts led to litigation with Sutton's chief proprietor, Sir Montagu Roger Burgoyne, from which Free emerged the loser.[53] 'The Parish knew that he was wrong, and many told him so', deposed John Northfield, 'but he would not hearken to reason.'[54]

His attitude towards the timber growing on the glebe had also led, of course, to trouble with his patron, St John's College, as recounted earlier . This timber was described by Montagu Burgoyne, in his petition to Parliament in 1825, as 'a fine Plantation of thriving Oaks of Sixty Years Growth, planted by One of his Predecessors'.[55]

His grasping nature showed up also in his attitude to tithes. The

51 LPL, H427/56, fos 63r and v, 78v, 127r.
52 St John's College, MS L10 (v).
53 LPL, H427/56, fos 63v, 127r.
54 Ibid., fol. 79r.
55 *LJ*, 57, p. 1111.

grassland that was tithable if tilled belonged to Sir John Burgoyne, who had allowed some of the poorer families in the village to have allotments on it on which they grew potatoes. The Rector compelled some of these poor folk to pay tithes on their potatoes. They, John Northfield recounted, thought it 'cruel conduct' and gave up growing such crops rather than continue to meet Free's demands.[56]

These demands seem to have stretched also to the very garden produce of the poor. The eighty year old Robert Oake 'kept a little bit of garden' wherein he grew a few potatoes and turnips. Dr Free demanded his portion of these, as he did also on at least one occasion of those of the widow Smith, despite the fact that she had been left with nine children to support.[57]

The physical state of the church gave rise to concern from time to time, though the need for repairs to be undertaken was to be expected in any building of this age. Not all of the repairs that the building underwent, however, were thought to be necessary. This applied particularly to the new roof put on to the chancel in 1820. Before this it was covered in lead, 'thick fine lead, wanting no repair', attested William Dennis, a young Potton bricklayer employed by Free to put slates on in its place. Nicholas Brown, William Dennis's uncle, was a building tradesman from Potton employed by Dr Free to do occasional jobs. He finished the slating that his nephew had begun. Brown saw the lead that had been removed: 'stout lead' that weighed over sixty-four hundredweight, he thought, and was worth perhaps £50. John Miller, the Potton plumber and glazier who stripped the lead off for the Rector, supported opinions about the quality of that which was removed. 'The lead was good to all appearance', he deposed: 'it had not been laid on more than fifty years.' There were perhaps a few repairs required, but Miller attested that he would have been prepared to do them for £5. As it was he took off, he thought, about £30 to £40 worth of lead, and the slating cost perhaps half as much. The lead, Brown tells

56 LPL, H427/56, fos 77v–78r.
57 Ibid., fos 110r, 115r.

us, was sold to someone in Cambridge. Dr Free was eventually charged with stripping the roof without lawful authority and converting the net proceeds to his own use.[58]

Of much greater concern to many in the community was the state of the churchyard. The Rector possessed a stock of animals, a stock that constantly changed in composition, but equally constantly required feeding. Witness after witness testified to his practice of allowing them to run loose in the churchyard. 'He had commonly one or two horses and several pigs there', stated William Hale, who had worked for Free as a lad, 'and at times, especially when the weather was any wise wet, the church yard was like a ploughed field.' He claimed never to have seen it free from pigs, 'running about and ... rooting up the graves'. When his father was interred 'Horses, cows and pigs were all there'.[59] Hales's brother John supported him: 'it was shameful to look at; not a grave was in decent order; the swine had rooted them up'. He could not find the grave of his father, 'buried but a few years before'.[60] Although the Rector claimed that the pigs crept into the churchyard through a hole in the wall, the testimony of others, and particularly of those who had worked for him, was damning. James Steers worked for Free from August 1822 to May 1823 and he deposed that:

> Doctor Free kept while the deponent was with him, a mare, a cow, a calf, a sow and pigs. He sold off most of the pigs as they grew to be porkers, weighing about eight or ten stone. All ... were turned into the church yard in the day time ... The deponent by his orders turned them in commonly every morning, and there they were fed. There were troughs in the church yard and the cattle always foddered there, on the one side or the other as the wind might be. In winter time the horse, cow and sheep were all foddered there; and at night the church porch was littered down for the sheep. The deponent has also foddered the horse and

58   Ibid., fos 41r and v, 136r and v, 142v; H427/55, p. 8.
59   LPL, H427/56, fos 16v–17r.
60   Ibid., fol. 26r.

cow there and left them there for the night ... The pigs were never left in the church yard after dark ... The deponent has seen the graves routed a good deal by the pigs and sow, and the cattle trod them in too ... Once the deponent looked down a hole and saw the nails on a coffin. The deponent many times shovelled the earth together and put it smooth ... Before Sunday came the deponent always shovelled away the dung from the pathway and cleaned out the porch; the rest of the church yard he raked about once in three or four weeks.[61]

The widow Phoebe Smith 'cried to see that sow muzzling about the graves, because she had two children buried there', and 'she cannot say where one of them lies as the mound has gone'.[62]

Many of the graves were unmarked because of the Rector's attitude towards gravestones. Scarcely any have been erected in Dr Free's time, deposed John Bowyer, 'for he insists on his right to charge what he pleases', an opinion supported by the widow Mary Hale.[63]

It is, therefore, hardly surprising that the numbers of those attending services at Sutton church soon fell away. The villagers saw what sort of clergyman they had been lumbered with and voted with their feet. Some gave up going to church at all, others went to Potton church or to the Methodist meeting house there. Maria Mackenzie stated of Sutton church that 'there were seldom more than two or three persons there attending divine service', and the ex-Churchwarden, William Cooper, told the Court of Arches that 'no one in the parish attends ... except an old man or woman or two who cannot get anywhere else'.[64] As witness after witness confirmed these statements we discover who some of the attenders were. Robert Oake was one. He went to Sutton church 'because

---

61 Ibid., fos 70r and v.
62 Ibid., fol. 114r.
63 Ibid., fos 100v, 125r.
64 Ibid., fol. 52v. Maria Mackenzie's statement is in the unpaginated section at the beginning of H427/56.

he is too infirm to get over to Potton'. Although she was much younger than Oake, Amy Randall was another attender. Her problem was 'that when she is in a church that is hot and crowded, she is subject to fits'. Sutton church was never crowded. Phoebe Smith, the widow with nine surviving children, went there 'for the most part in winter, because having so many children to look after she cannot go to Potton'. Very occasionally a few inquisitive children might attend.[65]

Absenteeism and a sullen hostility were the weapons that the inhabitants of Sutton chiefly employed against their detested minister. Given Free's iniquities, they also showed a remarkable tolerance. In 1823, however, events took a new turn. The leading inhabitants paraded his sins before the ecclesiastical authorities and embarked upon his prosecution. How and why this change occurred will be examined next.

65   Ibid., fos 105v, 109v, 116r.

4

Battling with the Burgoynes

D R Free was in some ways peculiarly democratic. Although he was clearly an impossibly arrogant and deceitful man, he did not reserve his high-handedness and deceptions for the poor and the weak; he was just as inclined to offend and cheat the rich and the powerful. He could probably have continued for the rest of his life to insult the ordinary parishioners of Sutton, those cottagers and labourers that made up the bulk of its population. They would have despised him, gossiped about him, and refused to attend his church, as clearly they did. They may even, as individuals, have launched prosecutions against him for debt or assault. Some also did this. But they were unlikely collectively to have made complaints to those in authority over him. They would have lacked the knowledge and the organisational skills that were necessary. Such initiatives would have to come, if they came at all, from the leading figures in the community.

The Rector clearly offended many of Sutton's farmers, and there are signs that they were not prepared to accept for ever his appalling behaviour. William Cooper, as we have noted, presented the Bishop of Lincoln in 1814 with the copy of the bastardy examination of Catharine Siggins that he had travelled to Hertford to obtain.[1] Nothing, however, seems to have come of such complaints. Nine years were to elapse before the ecclesiastical authorities were again warned that Dr Free was guilty of 'divers gross and heavy

---

1 See above, Chapter 2, pp. 22–23; see also frontispiece.

misdemeanors'. First of all complaints were made in writing by the
'parish officers' to the Bishop of Lincoln in January 1823; this was
followed by complaints made verbally to the Archdeacon of Bedford
in the April following; this in turn led to formal written presentments
of various charges being laid at the Archdeacon's Court at Bedford
in October 1823. These presentments were signed by eight individuals. They included William Cooper, then the Churchwarden;
William Coxall, the Assistant Churchwarden; at least two other
farmers, John Bowyer and Thomas Brown; William Masters, the
Overseer of the Poor; and John Northfield, the Constable of Sutton.
Northfield was not able to sign the presentments himself since he
could not write. Indeed he could barely read, a surprising inability
in someone who had once been Parish Clerk. As he admitted in
a deposition: 'he can read writing, but not very well'. Northfield's
name was signed for him by Montagu Burgoyne, whose name lurks
in the middle of the list and who was undoubtedly the organiser
of these presentments.[2] Dr Free was ill-advised to antagonise, as he
did from virtually the time of his arrival, the Burgoyne family, the
proprietors of Sutton, and his biggest mistake was to make an enemy
of Montagu Burgoyne.

The Burgoyne family had connections with Sutton that stretched
back at least as far as the sixteenth century. By the eighteenth century
they owned the entire parish, with the exception of the rectorial
glebe. Until the mid eighteenth century they also owned the ad-
vowson, the right of presentation to the living, but this was bought
from them by St John's College sometime between 1731 and 1771.[3]
They were not substantial landowners by county standards, but they
were a proud family with strong traditions of public, and especially
military, service.[4] The family's box pews still sit in All Saints church,

2 LPL, H427/55, pp. 10–11; H427/56, fol. 77r.
3 *Victoria History of the Counties of England: Bedfordshire* (London, 1972), ii,
   p. 246.
4 In Thomas Batchelor, *General View of the Agriculture of the County of
   Bedford* (London, 1808), their estates are listed as being confined to
   Sutton. The Duke of Bedford, by comparison, had possessions in
   twenty-five Bedfordshire parishes, ibid., p. 17. David Hool has suggested

5. Sketch of Sutton Park, Bedfordshire, by Thomas Fisher (1772–?).
The house burnt down in 1825. (*Bedfordshire Record Office*)

overlooked by the Burgoyne funeral monuments that dominate its interior.

Sir John Burgoyne, the seventh baronet, of Sutton, was a professional soldier from an early age, reaching the rank of Major General after success on the battlefields of India.[5] He died in Madras in 1785 and was succeeded by his eldest son, Sir Montagu Roger Burgoyne.[6] He also pursued a military career and, like his father, he reached the rank of Major General, dying at his mother's house in London in August 1817 not long after his return to England

to me that it may indeed have been their lack of landed income that produced these military careers.

5 He should not be confused with his more famous uncle, that other General John Burgoyne, the commander who surrendered his troops to the American army at Saratoga in 1777.

6 The name Montagu came into the family via the marriage of the sixth baronet, Sir Roger Burgoyne, to Lady Frances Montagu, the eldest daughter of George, Earl of Halifax. She was the mother of Sir John Burgoyne, the seventh baronet, and of his brother Montagu Burgoyne.

from service in Gibraltar.[7] He, in turn, was succeeded by his eldest son, Sir John Montagu Burgoyne, the ninth baronet and another professional soldier frequently away from Sutton. He was not there, for example, when Sutton Park, the family mansion, was destroyed by fire in 1825.[8] With the frequent absences of successive heads of the family, responsibility for maintaining their interest in Sutton appears to have been assumed by Montagu Burgoyne, younger brother of the seventh baronet (Sir John Burgoyne), uncle of the eighth baronet (Sir Montagu Roger Burgoyne) and great-uncle of the ninth baronet (Sir John Montagu Burgoyne).

Born in 1750, Montagu Burgoyne progressed from Trinity Hall, Cambridge, to a sinecure in the Exchequer worth £1660 a year granted by his cousin, Lord North, the son of his mother's sister. After being granted in 1774 the 'Inspectorship of Duties upon Tea and Coffee in the Excise', a post worth a mere £400 a year, Burgoyne wrote 'This great act of kindness will enable me to go through life in a most easy comfortable manner'.[9] This he appears to have accomplished, for in addition to his government posts he married Elizabeth Harvey, who not only brought him a substantial dowry but who also later inherited her father's wealth. Montagu Burgoyne was able, as a consequence, to buy himself an estate at Mark Hall near Harlow in Essex, where he resided for many years, playing a prominent part in public life.[10]

---

7   *Dictionary of National Biography* (London, 1886), ed. L. Stephen [hereafter *DNB*], vii, pp. 339–40; and pp. 62, 64–65 below.

8   BRO, CRT 190/171(i): the entry in Sir John's diary for 3 March 1825 reads 'received an express to say that Sutton House was burnt to the ground. Went down there immediately, and found it totally destroyed. It has only last year been new roofed and thoroughly repaired'.

9   Bodleian Library, Oxford, MS North d. 15, fos 203–4.

10 On Burgoyne see *Gentleman's Magazine*, new series, 5 (1836), part 1, p. 550; *Annual Register for the Year 1836* (London, 1837), appendix, p. 194; *DNB*, vii, p. 344; *Alumni Cantabrigienses*, ed. J. A. Venn (Cambridge, 1940), part 2, i, p. 453. Burgoyne bought Mark Hall from William Lushington and in 1819 sold it to Richard Arkwright, son of the famous cotton-spinner, who acquired it for his son, the Reverend Joseph Arkwright. See F. G. Emmison, *Guide to the Essex Record Office*

Montagu Burgoyne possessed an enviable combination of wealth, leisure and intelligence. He had a restless energy that never really found a career or focus for its expression. This energy was exhibited in various ways. He maintained the family tradition of military service, involving himself in 1794, at the age of forty-four, in raising a regiment of cavalry in Essex.[11] By 1797 he was Colonel of the Loyal Essex Regiment of Fencible Cavalry, serving in Scotland. The perhaps over-zealous and over-scrupulous ways in which he superintended his men led to his facing retaliatory charges of embezzlement and peculation laid against him by some of his junior officers. These charges were largely dismissed in the general court martial that he faced in 1799, a result that owed much to his own skilful defence in the case.[12] By 1802 he had resigned his sinecure at the Board of Excise and in the next eight years made several attempts to become one of the Members of Parliament for the county of Essex, but he failed to get himself elected.[13] He also had

(Chelmsford, 1969), p. 148. Burgoyne also possessed a house in Gloucester Place, London.

11 Essex Record Office, Chelmsford [hereafter ERO], S/U1/1.

12 Burgoyne's rejoinder to the prosecution at his court martial summed up the case presented against him. 'I am charged', he said, 'as Colonel of my Regiment with having embezzled the King's money, in purchasing horses for my Regiment at inferior prices to the regulation. I am charged with having embezzled the King's money in the allowance for the food of the horses of my Regiment. I am charged with various other transgressions of an inferior nature: in the two first charges I am accused of peculation and fraud respecting the mounting of the Regiment, and the care of those horses.' *Proceedings of a General Court Martial, Held in Barracks of Dublin, for the Trial of Col. Montague Burgoyne, of the Loyal Essex Regiment of Fencible Cavalry on Charges Preferred against Him by Major Crosse, and Captains Bund and Graham of the Same Regiment* (London, 1800), p. 289. In the event, Burgoyne was found not guilty of most of the charges, but guilty of taking two horses for his own use, and of withholding a small sum from the Quartermaster. Apart from the court's reprimand, no further action was taken against him.

13 Anon., *A Letter to the Freeholders of Essex, Occasioned by a Public Address to Them, Dated the 22nd of May, 1802, and Signed Montagu Burgoyne; by a Brother Freeholder* (London, 1802); Montagu Burgoyne, *A Letter from Montagu Burgoyne, Esquire, of Mark Hall, on the Present State of Public*

strong philanthropic interests. Correspondence survives with many of the leading figures of the day. One finds him begging statistics of grain exports from the farming expert Arthur Young in 1808, and asking for his opinion about the social impact of land enclosures on the poor. 'Nothing', Burgoyne wrote, 'can make amends for these pernicious consequences.'[14] 1814 saw him deeply involved in raising money, through a committee of subscribers, for 'ameliorating the situation of the Irish poor in this metropolis [London] and educating their children'. This education was not to extend, however, to interference with their religion.[15] The education of poor children remained an abiding interest. Burgoyne was an energetic and capable public figure, a zealous letter-writer to the press and a vigorous pamphleteer. He was clearly a crusader looking for a crusade: he was certainly not a man to be crossed.

Dr Free lost little time, however, in upsetting the Burgoynes. His attempt soon after his arrival to extend the boundaries of his glebe brought him into legal conflict with the eighth baronet, Sir Montagu Roger Burgoyne. William Coxall described how 'Dr Free tried to take possession of a Lane bounding his Glebe, and which he took in throwing down the fence; and he did the same with a Willow Row'.[16]

The Burgoynes also resented the tendency of the Rector and his cronies to poach on their land. In September 1814 Sir Montagu Roger Burgoyne alerted the Biggleswade magistrate Samuel Whitbread to the existence of a basket of game that Dr Free had sent for dispatch to London via the local coach office, the White Swan at Biggleswade. This game, Burgoyne suspected, had been poached

Affairs, and the Representation of the County of Essex (London, 1808); idem, *A Letter from Montagu Burgoyne, Esq. of Mark Hall, to the Freeholders and Inhabitants of the County of Essex, on the Present State of Public Affairs, and the Pressing Necessity of a Reform in the Commons House of Parliament* (London, 1809).

14 British Library, London [hereafter BL], MS Add. 35130, fos 21–22.
15 LPL, Fulham Papers (Howley), 9, fos 24–26, 28, 30–32.
16 LPL, H427/56, fol. 63v.

6. Montagu Burgoyne (1769–1821). Chalk and pencil drawing, heightened with white, by Henry Edridge. Dated 1818.

off his land, on which the Rector and a companion had been seen shooting recently. A search warrant was duly granted and two hares, two partridges and a pheasant were found awaiting carriage and impounded. Free's response to this was utterly characteristic: threatening to pursue the owner of the White Swan with litigation for the detention of the game, which he claimed was the property of his friend, he enquired of Whitbread whether he, the magistrate, had indeed ordered its detention. Ever tactful, the Rector added, 'Justice is administered in so peculiar a manner in this neighbourhood that I wish to ascertain whether your name in this instance is used with permission, as the gentleman will naturally expect to receive his own property directed by himself with legal authority'.[17] Although we do not know how this affair was settled, it can have done little to improve relationships between Sutton's main landlord and its priest.

Three years later, in 1817, the Rector attempted to get his revenge, and he did so in the most extraordinary way. Using a long-disused statute of 1581 designed by Elizabethan Protestants to secure the church attendance of Catholic Recusants and other Dissenters, Dr Free prosecuted Sir Montagu Roger Burgoyne at the Bedfordshire Lent Assizes for failing to attend church services at Sutton church over a period of nineteen months, attempting to extract from him the stipulated penalty of £20 per month and thus a total sum of £380.[18] The court, it was reported, was crowded almost to suffocation point, and the Rector, dressed in his canonicals, began by conducting his own case, until he was reminded by the Judge that matters should be left to his counsel. Margaret Johnston, his housekeeper at that time, was paraded as a witness to attest that from April 1815 to April 1816 she had attended church at Sutton

---

17 *Samuel Whitbread's Notebooks*, ed. Cirket, p. 123 (Sir Montagu Roger Burgoyne is here erroneously identified as Sir John Burgoyne); BRO, W1 315.

18 The case is reported in *The Times*, 17 March 1817, p. 3, and the *Annual Register for the Year 1817* (London, 1818), 59, pp. 192–96.

every Sunday without ever seeing Burgoyne there. This story was supported by John Northfield, then Parish Clerk of Sutton.

The credibility of these statements was questioned, however, by Burgoyne's counsel, Serjeant Blossett. Church attendance every Sunday for a year would have been difficult given that the church was shut up, with no services at all being provided, from June to early September in that year. For this shameful neglect of his duties, Blossett asserted, Dr Free had received a 'monition', a formal warning, from the Bishop of Lincoln. Even when the Rector was in residence, Blossett continued, his parishioners were never sure at what time services would be held, or indeed whether they would be held at all. He continued by pointing out that Sir Montagu Burgoyne had other reasons for not attending the parish church. When he did go he was liable to suffer tirades of personal abuse from the pulpit instead of sermons 'inculcating divine truths'. Even apart from this, his health prevented regular attendance. Sir Montagu, he reminded the jury, was a British General who had returned to England in poor health in 1814 after service in Gibraltar, a statement that was later supported by a physician brought forward by Blossett as one of a string of defence witnesses. Others included the Reverend Dr Hughes, a clerical visitor to Sutton Park, and a domestic servant there, both of whom testified to the regularity of family prayers on those occasions when Sir Montagu did not venture to church. Two Churchwardens of Sutton, Thomas Brown and Lawrence Coxall, confirmed that their parish church was indeed shut up from 25 June to 3 September and again from 15 September to 5 November.[19] The jury had no hesitation in finding Sir Montagu not guilty.

The monition that Sergeant Blossett referred to probably lies behind the letter that Dr Free wrote to his ecclesiastical masters at Lincoln in February 1816, notifying them that he was absent from Sutton from the 26 June to 7 September 1815 'to take the benefit of the mineral waters, the church being shut up for necessary repairs during the same period', and that he was absent again 'upon urgent

---

19 Lawrence Coxall was William Coxall's father.

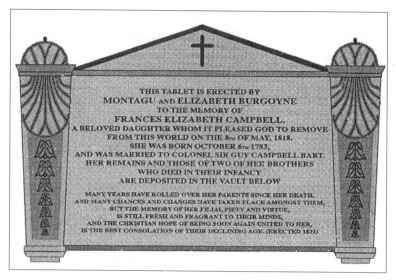

THIS TABLET IS ERECTED BY
MONTAGU AND ELIZABETH BURGOYNE
TO THE MEMORY OF
FRANCES ELIZABETH CAMPBELL.
A BELOVED DAUGHTER WHOM IT PLEASED GOD TO REMOVE
FROM THIS WORLD ON THE 8TH OF MAY, 1818.
SHE WAS BORN OCTOBER 6TH 1783,
AND WAS MARRIED TO COLONEL SIR GUY CAMPBELL BART.
HER REMAINS AND THOSE OF TWO OF HER BROTHERS
WHO DIED IN THEIR INFANCY
ARE DEPOSITED IN THE VAULT BELOW

MANY YEARS HAVE ROLLED OVER HER PARENTS SINCE HER DEATH,
AND MANY CHANCES AND CHANGES HAVE TAKEN PLACE AMONGST THEM,
BUT THE MEMORY OF HER FILIAL PIETY AND VIRTUE,
IS STILL FRESH AND FRAGRANT TO THEIR MINDS,
AND THE CHRISTIAN HOPE OF BEING SOON AGAIN UNITED TO HER,
IS THE BEST CONSOLATION OF THEIR DECLINING AGE. (ERECTED 1831)

7. Recreation of Burgoyne memorial tablet, All Saints, Sutton.

business' from 13 October to 16 November 1815.[20] To attempt in 1817 to prosecute the lord of the manor for failing to attend weekly church services from April 1815 to April 1816 reveals either extra-ordinary forgetfulness on the Rector's part or equally extraordinary duplicity.

Any pleasure Sir Montagu derived from his success at the Bedford Assizes could not have lasted long, since his poor health caught up with him and he died at his mother's house in London in August 1817.[21] Indeed, deaths amongst the Burgoynes appear to have precipitated the next crisis in their relations with Dr Free. In May 1818 Frances Elizabeth, the elder of Montagu Burgoyne's two surviving children, died. She was in Italy at the time and had been married to Lieutenant-Colonel Sir Guy Campbell for little more than a year.[22] Heartbroken by this, Burgoyne arranged to have her body brought back to Sutton for burial, despite the fact that he

20 Lincolnshire Archives, Lincoln (hereafter LA), NER 1816/12.
21 *Gentleman's Magazine*, 87 (1817), part 2, p. 189.
22 Ibid., part 1, p. 178. Her death is recorded in the memorial tablet in Sutton church erected by her father in 1831.

was then still living at Mark Hall in Essex. Sutton was where the
Burgoynes tended to be interred, as the many monuments in the
church attest, and Montagu Burgoyne had already buried two of
his children there. After the death of Frances her father's thoughts
clearly turned to these earlier deaths in his family. He applied to
the Bishop of Lincoln for permission to remove the bodies of the
two children, who had died about twenty years previously, from
the family vault in Sutton church 'to another family vault recently
erected' by him in Sutton church.[23] The building of this new vault,
created for Frances, was the event that turned Montagu Burgoyne,
who had previously shown little interest in Sutton's troubles, into
the Rector's most implacable enemy.

The testimonies of several witnesses in the Court of Arches in
1828 throw light on what happened. William Cooper recollected
having heard that Dr Free had made Montagu Burgoyne pay a
hundred guineas for burying his daughter in a vault under Sutton
church.[24] James Steers also deposed that 'it was the report all round
the country that Doctor Free had made Mr Burgoyne pay an
hundred guineas for leave to make a vault to bury his daughter
who had been brought from Italy'.[25] An additional reason for
Burgoyne's anger is suggested by the testimony of William Coxall.
He recounted the same story of the Rector insisting on this payment
for the interment of Frances, but added, 'and that he [Free] had
made the family pay the like sum for leave to make a vault under
Sutton church some time previously for Sir Montagu Burgoyne'.
Adding authenticity to this story, Coxall stated that this had been
told him by Sir John Burgoyne.[26]

23 LA, FB4/140b.
24 LPL, H427/56, fol. 54v.
25 Ibid., fol. 71r.
26 Ibid., fol. 63v. The story is supported also by Mary Hale's testimony,
    ibid., fol. 101v: 'The respondent believes that the said Doctor Free did
    compel Mr Burgoyne ... to pay one hundred guineas for leave to make
    a vault in which to bury Mr Burgoyne's daughter, having himself
    received the same sum for leave to make a vault for Sir Montagu
    Burgoyne some time previously.'

Dr Free certainly convinced himself that Montagu Burgoyne's enmity derived from the vault episode. To the Bishop of London in May 1828 he wrote that 'Because I charged Mr Montague Burgoyne, late of Mark Hall, Essex (but now of East Sheen), more for a vault at Sutton, Bedfordshire (where he has no property), than he expected, he has ever since been propagating the basest and unfounded reports ... and has so far succeeded as to prejudice the legal authorities against my having that protection which the law holds out even if the allegations were true'.[27] He was later to argue that Burgoyne had vowed to ruin him, 'to strip the gown from his back', even if it cost him £20,000, and had hired 'spies and emissaries' to watch his every move, even following him to London in the hope of catching him in some scandalous episode, which could be used against him.[28] Burgoyne was certainly capable of such planning. Concerned about poaching in the neighbourhood of his Essex home, he arranged in 1817 for a London Bow Street officer called Ruthven to lodge at a local public house and to put the word about that he wished to purchase some game. Contact was made with a man called Williams, who introduced Ruthven to Daniel Farrow and James Cass. An arrangement was made that they should raid a neighbouring gentleman's wood on the night of 10 January, and it was there that Farrow and Cass were arrested by Burgoyne and an armed party, forewarned about the raid.[29]

Dr Free's outrageous behaviour appears to have caught up with him in 1823 when a series of written complaints were made in January by the parish officers and others to the Bishop of Lincoln.[30] They were then made verbally to the Archdeacon of Bedford, who visited Sutton on 18 June, probably by William Cooper who was

---

27 LPL, Fulham Papers (Howley), 16, fol. 208.
28 These accusations were implied in the 'interrogatories' put to witnesses on Free's behalf at his trial in the Court of Arches. See LPL, H427/56, fos 54v–55r.
29 *The Times*, 17 March 1817, p. 3.
30 This is alleged in the two presentments made to the Archdeacon's Court in October 1823. See Appendix 2 below, pp. 145–48.

sworn in as Churchwarden on that occasion.[31] This must have provoked bad feeling with the Rector, because William Cooper, William Coxall and Thomas Ashton, all of Sutton, were bound in a recognisance by the Justices in July 1823 to appear at the next Bedford Quarter Sessions and enjoined to keep the peace 'and particularly towards Edward Drax Free, Doctor in Divinity'.[32] Meanwhile the complaints made to the Bishop and Archdeacon began to take effect. William Cooper was summoned to appear at the Bishop's Palace at Buckden in August, and it was subsequently decided by the ecclesiastical authorities that these complaints should be put formally to the Archdeacon sitting in court at Bedford.[33] On 24 October two 'presentments' were put formally to that body by William Cooper.[34] 'We, the churchwarden, overseer, constable, and parishioners of Sutton ...', the first of these two presentments began, 'do present, that our Rector, the Reverend Dr Free, has been guilty of divers misdemeanors.' There then followed a list of complaints, accusing Free of having demanded fees for baptism, and refusing to baptise without them; of neglecting to offer divine services; of desecrating the churchyard with his livestock; of refusing the vestry the use of the church and the Churchwarden access to the register; of disturbing the peace; of selling lead off the church roof to his 'pecuniary advantage'; and of being absent from Sutton since 17 August 'on account of a warrant with which the constable endeavoured to arrest him'. The second presentment accused the Rector of inebriety; of leading 'an immoral and incontinent life'; and of being guilty of 'swindling and shop-lifting'.[35]

Although by 1828 William Cooper, whose name headed the presentments of 1823, claimed not to recall who had actually drawn up and prepared these two documents, he was prepared to admit

31 Ibid.; BRO, ABC/17, p. 17.
32 BRO, QSR 1823/197.
33 BRO, ABCP 391/1–3.
34 BRO, ABC/17, p. 131v.
35 LPL, H427/55, pp. 10–11. These two presentments are reproduced in Appendix 2 below.

that 'Montagu Burgoyne procured it to be done from the information which was communicated to him'.[36] William Coxall's memory was a little better. He thought that the two documents may have been written by Mr Wenham, Sir John Burgoyne's estate Steward. He remembered that those who signed met on two or three occasions to formulate their complaints, and that they were signed in a morning session at the Park Cottage. Coxall was not prepared to admit that Montagu Burgoyne had played an especially active part, since the parishioners had already resolved to complain about Dr Free, but, he added, 'perhaps as Mr Burgoyne knew better than they did how it was proper to proceed, these presentments might not have been made as they were, and when they were, had not Mr Burgoyne interfered ...'[37] John Northfield, another of the signatories, was more positive: he remembered that 'Mr Burgoyne ... did take an active part in getting those presentments made', and that it was Burgoyne, or his Bedford attorney, Mr Budd, who asked him to put his name to them.[38]

At some point, hard to pin down with precision, Montagu Burgoyne began to collect evidence of the Rector's misbehaviour. Soon after Maria Mackenzie left Free's service in April or May 1823, and whilst she was still living in Sutton, she was summoned to the 'Great House', Sutton Park, where she was interviewed by Montagu Burgoyne in company with the Archdeacon of London whom he had brought there. They apparently asked her whether she had been living with the Rector, and whether she had been put in 'the family way' by him: to both questions, she answered that she had.[39] Later, some time after February 1824, she was summoned to Bedford by Budd, the attorney who had quashed Free's attempt to settle with Maria Mackenzie. Budd arranged for her to make affidavits before several London solicitors.[40] We have

---

36 LPL, H427/56, fol. 55r.
37 Ibid., fol. 64v.
38 Ibid., fol. 79v.
39 Ibid., fos 9r and v.
40 Ibid., fos 7r–8v.

already seen that Burgoyne also visited Margaret Johnston's sister, Mary Johnston, in Somers Town in the summer of 1823 or 1824 (she could not by 1828 recollect exactly which year it was), enquiring about the illegitimate child that Free had lodged with her.[41] Eliza Pierson remembered being summoned by Burgoyne in or around 1824 to a meeting in his house in Gloucester Place, London. He must already have known where she was living: Eliza had left Sutton in 1823, having stayed there for only a few weeks. By 1828, however, he had lost track of her: he had to advertise in the London papers for her to get in touch with the Proctor who was handling the prosecution of Free in Doctors' Commons.[42] John Northfield swore in 1828 that he knew nothing about Burgoyne having Dr Free watched and followed, but he did admit that three or four years before, when there were to be two christenings in the church, Burgoyne sent him 'to see and bring him word what passed and how Dr Free behaved'.[43] Bringing Burgoyne word was now much easier, because he began to spend much more time in Sutton. Until 1825 he might have stayed in the family home at Sutton Park,[44] but when that house burned down he had to find alternative accommodation. The arrangement that he made was to rent two rooms in the farmhouse of the widow Munn and, in this way, to become a nominal resident of the parish. This, in turn, enabled him to become in 1824 Churchwarden of Sutton, a modest position for a man of his elevated social status, but one that he was anxious to occupy and one that the villagers were pleased to see him occupying.[45] The nominal reason for this was, as one witness testified

41 See above, Chapter 2. Burgoyne certainly knew where she lived by November 1823 and that she had one of Free's children living with her, BRO, ABCP 391/16.
42 LPL, H427/56, fol. 44v.
43 Ibid., fol. 79r.
44 Although it appears to have been leased to a branch of the family of the Russells, Dukes of Bedford, for a time.
45 Four years later he was still being elected as the Churchwarden. William Cooper provides a vivid little picture of his election in 1828. On the day announced for the meeting of the Vestry and election of the Church-

in 1828, 'to enable him the better to regulate and improve the parish, by building a school and otherwise'.[46] Burgoyne kept his word. John Northfield told the court in 1828 that 'He has erected a school room in the parish for boys, and another for girls; and as he pays a good deal of attention to them; he sometimes occupies his aforesaid lodging'.[47]

The real reason, however, was that the prosecution of Dr Free in the ecclesiastical courts required a nominal prosecutor, someone required 'to promote the office of the judge'. The original intentions of the ecclesiastical officers at Bedford and Buckden was that the case should be promoted by William Cooper, the Churchwarden at that time, a responsibility that Cooper would have been only too happy to hand over to Montagu Burgoyne.[48] The latter had been doing his homework. It was Burgoyne, and not William Cooper, who in November 1823 sent Charles Bailey, the Deputy Registrar at Bedford, a list of witnesses required to substantiate the charges against Dr Free, a list that contained the names and addresses of a number of key participants. Margaret Johnston and Maria Mackenzie, both with addresses in Somers Town, were on the list, as also was Ann Taylor ('now at Mrs Wisbey's Sidcup house'). Others, such as Maria Crook and Catharine Siggins, were there, but their whereabouts were not known.

At this stage the Rector was in serious trouble. He sensed it. He thought about exchanging livings, escaping his persecutors by

---

warden, the members were all busy attending a sale in the village. Cooper, who was also there, urged them to leave the sale and attend the meeting, but they would not. They all agreed, however, to Burgoyne being their Churchwarden, telling Cooper that 'they would sign the book another time'. Cooper went to the church, where the Parish Clerk, William Bunting was present, and told him that the parish was nominating Burgoyne. Bunting asked whether he should call Dr Free, and Cooper replied to the effect that he would sooner see the Devil himself, LPL, H427/56, fos 58v–59r.

46 Ibid., fol. 127v.
47 Ibid., fol. 79v.
48 BRO, ABCP 391/10.

moving elsewhere. A clergyman from Hull, corresponding with the Reverend Mr Williamson of Campton, Bedfordshire, wrote early in January 1824:

> When you write again tell me what you know of Dr Free of Sutton. He applied to me about an exchange of livings here in Hull; but I thought him rather eccentric in his conduct. I have, therefore, declined having any further communication.[49]

Even before the presentments were made, at the court session held in Bedford on 24 October, Free had instructed his London solicitors, Messrs Croft and Johnson, to intercede with the ecclesiastical authorities there on his behalf. He also wrote directly to them himself. These letters do not survive, but from the reply drafted by Richard Smith, the Bishop of Lincoln's Commissary at Buckden, it would appear that Free had intimated that he was prepared to put in a Curate at Sutton to halt the proceedings against him.[50] Smith advised that this should be done without delay because, once the Archdeacon began to try the accusations that were being made, he could not see how the proceedings could be halted.[51] No one at this stage could foresee how matters were to develop, and Smith was probably not alone in underestimating the cunning and ingenuity of the slippery Rector of Sutton. The trials of Dr Free were poised to begin – in more senses than one.

---

49 BRO, M 10/5/164.
50 It was alleged in the Commons in 1825 that 'Mr Burgoyne had acted with the greatest reluctance, and had given Dr Free the option to give up his Rectory and appoint a curate, and then no public notice would be taken of his conduct', BRO, LL 17/330/2.
51 LPL, H427/22.

5

The Trials of Dr Free

Doubt and indecision characterised the prosecution of Dr Free from the outset. He was perhaps fortunate in that the ecclesiastical machinery under which he was to be tried was extraordinarily complicated, consisting as it did of a multitude of overlapping and sometimes competing jurisdictions. As Lord Chancellor Cottenham explained to the Lords in 1839, 'besides those superior courts [those of the Archbishops and Bishops], nearly 300 other ecclesiastical courts were in existence'.[1] It was also a machine that, at the local level at least, was rusty through lack of use. By the early nineteenth century the local ecclesiastical courts, such as those of the Archdeacons, met infrequently and conducted a small volume of mostly routine church business. Local officials were clearly uncertain, when highly unusual cases such as Dr Free's came their way, about the procedures that were involved, in what courts prosecutions could be pursued, and what offences could actually be punished. All of these features are observable in the early stages of this case, bearing out Cottenham's complaint that 'One great misfortune was, that nobody knew which court had jurisdiction and which had not; it was impossible for the parties to discover in which court they should institute proceedings'.[2]

Charles Bailey, the Archdeaconry Registrar at Bedford, had on 7 October 1823 to tell his Deputy Registrar precisely what was

1 T. C. Hansard, *Parliamentary Debates* [hereafter *PD*], 3rd series, 47, col. 1308.
2 Ibid.

expected of him when the presentments of the Churchwardens of Sutton were laid before the forthcoming court. 'The Archdeacon being seated at the visitation', he wrote, 'the presentment is given to you, and you then ask the Churchwardens if that is a true presentment by virtue of the oath they have taken.' He reminded the official to bring the Visitation Book with him, and to make entry in the form that he then demonstrated. 'If after the presentment is given in', he continued,

> the Churchwardens mean to follow up such presentment by instituting a cause against Dr Free, they must ask leave of the Chancellor of Lincoln, in whose court I presume the cause must be instituted, and upon his giving them leave, they enter into a bond in a penalty of £100 to exonerate him, the Chancellor, from all expenses as the suit must be carried on in his name, you not being able to entertain a suit of this nature in the Archdeacon's court.[3]

After at least one postponement, the Archdeacon's Court met on 24 October and received the presentments against the Rector of Sutton.[4] Then the archdeaconry officials anxiously pondered the next steps they should take. Despite Bailey's advice that actions of this sort could not be pursued in his court, the Archdeacon, Henry Kaye Bonney, seemed to be prepared to go ahead with a prosecution. On 13 November he sent Bailey instructions that 'the office of the judge' was to be promoted by William Cooper, Churchwarden, before 'Henry Kaye Bonney, D.D., Archdeacon of Bedford'.[5] Ten days before this he had begged Bailey to let him know the name of the Proctor he was thinking of employing for the prosecution, offering him the opinion that 'a proctor conversant in such cases is now of rare occurrence'. Bonney also foresaw some of the difficulties that lay ahead:

Remember that the refusing to pay workmen and shoplifting

3 BRO, ABCP 391/3.
4 BRO, ABC/17, p. 131v.
5 BRO, ABCP 391/9.

must not be put into the citation, neither must the incontinency, if it took place beyond 8 calendar months before the first commencement. The proctor who draws the citation ought to obtain the dates of all the offences stated to have been committed by Dr F.[6]

A statute of 1787, entitled 'An Act to Prevent Frivolous and Vexatious Suits in Ecclesiastical Courts', had laid down that suits for defamation could only be begun in any ecclesiastical court within six months of the slander having been been uttered, and no suit for fornication or incontinence, or for striking or brawling in any church or churchyard, could be commenced after a period of eight calendar months from the alleged offence.[7]

The Archdeacon also drew attention to certain procedural difficulties that lay ahead:

> I must direct your attention particularly to the commencement of the proceedings. The prosecution must be in the name of the Churchwarden. The citation must state specifically the charges and no other can be introduced into the articles. The citation and articles must agree in substance, and the articles must be ready by the second court day after the defendant appears, or by the course of practice he is intitled to be dismissed with costs.[8]

Ten days later, on 13 November, Bonney offered Bailey the fruits of his own enquiries into possible Proctors to pursue the prosecution. George Jenner, the Registrar of the Court of Arches, Messrs Shepherd and Isherwood, Registrars of the Consistory Court of London, and Mr Fox, the Registrar of the Commissary Court, were 'the most esteemed' and, unless Bailey had a Proctor that he usually employed, he would pick Fox.

William Fox was indeed chosen as Proctor and copies of the presentments, along with lists of possible witnesses were quickly

6 BRO, ABCP 391/8.
7 27 George III, c. 44, reproduced in Appendix 3 below, pp. 149–50.
8 BRO, ABCP 391/8.

sent off to him at Doctors' Commons in London.[9] His immediate response was that 'The instructions appear very imperfect as to dates', pointing out to Charles Bailey that he needed to be furnished with exact dates for all the different charges. Some of them, as he remarked, seem to go back to 1814, well out of time as far as the Act of 1787 was concerned. Fox also asked Bailey, 'Has your Archdeacon's court jurisdiction to sustain such a suit as this, which might lead to the suspension at least of a clergyman, or should not such suit be brought in the Bishop's court of the diocese?'[10]

The Archdeacon appears to have decided subsequently that he did not have the power to pursue Dr Free, and by the beginning of December the case had been transferred to the the Bishop of Lincoln's Commissary, Richard Smith, seemingly with the intent that it be prosecuted in the highest of all ecclesiastical courts, one where the existence of expertise was guaranteed, the Court of Arches in London.[11] The Bishop himself was meanwhile seeking opinions from these very experts. This forced Smith later that month to have to inform Montagu Burgoyne, Budd and Cooper that the Bishop's opinion was:

> in the case of Sutton parish versus Dr Free, it being the opinion of Dr Lushington and Mr Fox of Doctors' Commons that the principal charge of incontinency cannot be admitted and entertained; and the remaining charges being of such a nature as have been usually corrected by admonition of the Bishop himself, his Lordship will proceed to notice them in the usual manner, and therefore does not think it necessary to send them to the Court of Arches.

Evidently the Bishop was persuaded that it was not desirable to

---

9 Doctors' Commons was a group of buildings near to St Paul's Cathedral, housing the corporation of civil lawyers that practised in the Court of Arches, the Consistory Court of the Bishop of London, the Prerogative Court of Canterbury and the High Court of Admiralty.
10 Letter of 17 November 1823, BRO, ABCP 391/15.
11 BRO, ABCP 391/17, 2 December 1823.

incur the 'risque and expence of a Suit in the Arches', and William Fox was accordingly instructed to suspend proceedings.[12]

There is then an infuriating gap in the documentary evidence, so that we do not know how Burgoyne and the parishioners of Sutton reacted to the news that their Rector had apparently escaped serious punishment. It is likely, however, that this announcement spurred Burgoyne into even greater efforts to find hard evidence and to bring Free to court. Certainly by the autumn the ecclesiastical authorities at Lincoln had been persuaded by someone into a change of mind. Early in October 1824 the case of *Burgoyne* versus *Free* began its tortuous course in the Court of Arches before Sir John Nicholl, ironically a contemporary of Free's at St John's College, Oxford.

Proceedings commenced there on 14 October with William Fox, Burgoyne's Proctor, exhibiting to the court Letters of Request from Richard Smith, the Commissary of the Bishop of Lincoln in the Archdeaconry of Bedford, to try the cause promoted by Montagu Burgoyne, in the office of the judge, against the Reverend Dr Edward Drax Free.[13]

At the next meeting of the court, on the 9 November, the Proctors for both parties appeared: William Fox, acting for Burgoyne, and Richard Addams and Henry Whitfield Cresswell, acting for Free.[14] On this occasion, moreover, Cresswell entered a protest or objection to the case proceeding, on the purely legal grounds that the Letters of Request transferring the case to the Court of Arches had come from the wrong source: they should have come from the Bishop's Chancellor, William Battine, and not from the Bishop's Commissary, Richard Smith. Behind this lay the argument that the case should have been heard initially in the Bishop of Lincoln's Court.

---

12 BRO, ABCP 391/19, 26 December.
13 LPL, H427/2, 17. This and subsequent stages are conveniently summarised in the printed summary of the case prepared later for the Court of Delegates, LPL, H427/55.
14 LPL, H427/3.

Subsequent meetings of the Court of Arches led to the protest being 'extended', that is explained more fully; to Richard Smith's patent of office being examined to determine the exact nature of his powers; and eventually, in late January 1825, to this protest being overruled.[15]

It is significant that support for the objection came from Dr William Battine himself, evidence of the jealousies and tensions that were engendered by this complicated jurisdictional structure. His Proctor argued that the Letters of Request required Battine's permission and signature to go straight from the Commissary's Court to the Arches. It led Richard Smith to comment to Charles Bailey, 'You as well as myself will, I am sure, be glad to find that we can do without Mr Chancellor [Dr Battine] at Bedford, the Commissary's jurisdiction being decided to be concurrent with his'.[16]

Meanwhile, on 29 October, Dr Free had been served with the citation or summons to appear before the court to answer certain charges:

> touching and concerning his soul's health, and the lawful correction and reformation of his manners and excesses, but more especially for the crime of fornication or incontinence; for profane cursing and swearing, indecent conversation, drunkenness, and immorality; for his lewd and profligate life and conversation; for neglect of divine service on divers Sundays, using the porch of the church of the said parish

15 The basis of the objection was that the Letters of Request should follow the same legal route as appeals, and that in this case the Letters should have gone to the Bishop of Lincoln's court and not to the metropolitan court. The legal grounds for the objection, and those for its refusal, are summarised in Addams's report on the case, *English Reports*, 162, pp. 343–47. See also *The Times*, 18 February 1825, where the issues are clearly explained. Also William Fox's report to Richard Smith, BRO, ABCP 391/21: 'The judge said the words of your patent were very strong, that yours is an episcopal court, as well as the Chancellor's of the diocese, and that appeals lie from both courts to the Arches; that he considered Letters of Request to lie also equally from both courts ...'

16 BRO, ABCP 391/21.

as a stable, and foddering cattle therein, and turning out swine into the church-yard; for refusing the use of the said church for vestry meetings lawfully called; for converting to his own use and profit the lead on the roof of the chancel of the said church; for refusing, and neglecting, and delaying to baptise or christen divers children of his parishioners; for refusing and neglecting to bury sundry corpses, and for requiring illegal fees to be paid to him for baptisms and burials.

Dr Free was to appear before the court to answer 'certain articles or interrogatories to be exhibited against and administered to him'.[17]

At the next sitting of the court, early in February 1825, Fox submitted these Articles detailing the charges against Dr Free. This extraordinarily lengthy document contained no fewer than thirty-one points of argument and accusation.[18] Of these, the key ones turned out to be, as matters transpired, not those that detailed his sexual transgressions with a succession of named housekeepers, but the opening ones. The first of these reminded him that by the ecclesiastical laws of the Church of England ministers were required to be 'grave, decent, reverend, and orderly' and had to abstain from 'fornication or incontinence, profaneness, drunkenness, lewdness, profligacy, or any other excess whatsoever'. This was required of them 'under pain of deprivation of their ecclesiastical benefices, suspension from the exercise of their clerical functions, or such other ecclesiastical punishment ...' The second Article simply established that Free was a priest and had been legally admitted to his living at Sutton.

To these thirty-one Articles were appended five exhibits: the record of Free's admission to the Rectory; the bastardy examinations by magistrates of Maria Crook and Catharine Siggins; and the two presentments made to the Archdeacon of Bedford by the parish officers of Sutton.[19]

17 LPL, H427/55, pp. 3–4.
18 See below, Appendix 4, pp. 151–67.
19 LPL, H427/12.

Two weeks later the Judge, after hearing arguments from both sides, rejected the fourth and the twenty-first Articles that were submitted.[20] The reasons for this are not clear but may be that some charges were too general and lacked specificity. The fourth Article, for example, charged

> that since your institution and induction to the said rectory you have led an immoral and incontinent life, and have frequently committed the crime of fornication or incontinence; that you have been in the habit of keeping one female servant in the said rectory house, and of often changing such servant; and that on female servants first entering into your service, and coming to reside in your said house, you have solicited and urged them to commit fornication and incontinence with you; that on some of such servants refusing to comply with such your desires, you discharged them from your service, and that with others of such servants you formed and carried on a criminal intercourse and connection, and that they continued to live with you in the said house in a state of fornication and incontinence for a considerable time together; and this was true, public, and notorious ...

Sir John Nicholl, the presiding Judge, rejected the charge contained in the fifth Article that Free had tried to persuade Maria Crook to name one of his labourers as the father of her child. He rejected also the assertions in the eleventh Article that Free had a venereal disease which he had communicated to Maria Mackenzie, and that this was revealed by marks on his linen. Also rejected was the assertion in the thirteenth Article that Free had boasted to several of his housekeepers that he had had carnal connections with young girls not more than ten years of age. Such charges were largely based on hearsay and may also have been difficult to sustain after a lengthy lapse of time.

20 LPL, H427/8, 55, pp. 4–10. The rejections and alterations in the Articles are printed in Appendix 2 scored through. The version printed in Coote is the 'reformed' version.

Free's Proctors pleaded also for the rejection of all Articles in which it was claimed that the Rector was guilty of fornication, on the grounds that these alleged offences had occurred years before and were well out of time as far as the Act of 1787 was concerned. Sir John Nicholl, after considering positions from both sides, held that that statute had been brought in to protect laymen from vexatious litigation and that it was never intended to prevent prosecutions of clerics in respect of deprivation of office. He was prepared to allow the Articles in question, but he invited the defendant to test his interpretation of the 1787 Act by appealing to some other body or court.[21]

This advice was almost immediately followed and, although the case proceeded in stately fashion through various formal stages, in May 1825 the Registrar of the Court of Arches was served with a writ of prohibition that led to the case being halted whilst a ruling on the 1787 Act was obtained from the Court of King's Bench to which Dr Free had applied.[22]

Two years had elapsed since William Cooper and others had laid their complaints verbally before the Archdeacon of Bedford, and eighteen months of legal wrangling and consequent delays had followed the formal presentments of October 1823. It is not surprising, therefore, that Montagu Burgoyne's patience was running low. He expressed his exasperation in that petition of June 1825 to the House of Lords with which our story began. In language that was far from judicious, he rehearsed the complaints of the villagers against their minister, complaining of Free's 'incontinence, drunkenness, profane and indecent language, the omissions and negligences, the extortions and abuses in his discharge of his holy office'. None of this had, of course, yet been proved in a court of law. Arguing 'That after years of endurance, solicitation, suspense and disappointment, the petitioners are still told that they have an indefinite period of litigation before them', he pleaded for an

21 See the summary of these hearings in Addams's reports, *English Reports*, 162, pp. 347–48.
22 LPL, H427/55, p. 2.

amendment to the Act of 1787 to remove the protection it gave to scandalous clergy.[23]

Meanwhile Dr Free was not only still offending his parishioners, he was also continuing to make extra-legal efforts to get out of the predicament in which he had landed himself. In July 1825 the Reverend John Shephard, writing from Brussels, informed Charles Bailey that a month before this he had responded to an advertisement placed in the newspapers, by someone identifying himself as 'Verax', a 'Rector wishing to give up his house to any gentleman who would take charge of his living'. This had turned out to be Dr Free. Shephard had subsequently seen, however, a newspaper report occasioned by Burgoyne's petition to Parliament, and 'What I have seen in the papers makes me fearful of continuing a correspondence ...'[24]

The King's Bench judgement, when it came in May 1826, ruled that the Act of 1787 was not a bar to pursuing a clergyman on a charge of fornication, even if committed more than eight months previously, providing that deprivation of his living was the object of the prosecution and not 'reformation of manners or the soul's health', as would be the case if a non-cleric were being prosecuted, a layman having no living to lose. The King's Bench Judges were persuaded by the first two Articles of accusation, and the wide range of other offences with which the Rector had been charged, that this was indeed the objective of his prosecutors, and that the case could proceed on that basis.[25] Free was, however, initially awarded costs against Burgoyne, but this award was later rescinded because the prohibition that he obtained was only a partial one, not a complete one.[26]

Free and his lawyers responded to this by obtaining immediately a Writ of Error, appealing the judgement to the Exchequer Chamber. This turned out to be an error in itself, since the appeal should have

23 *LJ*, 57, pp. 1110–11.
24 BRO, ABA 6/25.
25 *English Reports*, 108, pp. 149–51; LPL, H427/55, p. 2.
26 This is explained in the petition made by Free to the House of Lords in May 1827: *LJ*, 59, p. 336; and in the report in *English Reports*, 108, p. 550.

been directed not to the Exchequer Chamber but to the House of Lords. Consequently Free's lawyers obtained a new writ appealing the judgement to the House of Lords, and in the process suspended once again the proceedings in the Court of Arches.[27] This effectively delayed matters through the summer to the autumn of 1826.

The period in which suspension was operative lapsed, however, without a further order to stay proceedings being received, and the Court of Arches resumed the business of *Burgoyne* versus *Free*. The Articles of accusation, as 'reformed', were admitted by Nicholl on 20 November. The consequence of this was that wherever it was explicitly stated in the Articles that Free was being charged with 'the crime of fornication and incontinence' it was struck out.[28]

At a subsequent session at the end of November 1826, however, Addams announced that he had appealed the case to the High Court of Delegates to examine the issues. The basis of Free's appeal was that the Judge, Sir John Nicholl, 'unduly and unjustly proceeding in the said cause' and 'too much favouring the part of the said Montagu Burgoyne', acted improperly in admitting certain of the Articles and in resuming the case whilst it was under appeal in the House of Lords.[29] By February 1827 the case was once more suspended in the Court of Arches.[30]

27 *English Reports*, 108, pp. 285, 363; LPL, H427/55, p. 2.
28 See Appendix 4.
29 See the 'Inhibition and Citation', dated 1 February 1827, and the 'Second Article of the Libel of Appeal' printed in LPL, H427/55, pp. 14–16, which states that Free conceived himself 'to be injured and aggrieved by certain grievances, nullities and iniquities, injustices and injuries, as well by virtue of the said Judge's pretended office, as at the unjust instance, instigation, solicitation, procurement, and petition of the said Montagu Burgoyne, or his proctor, by the said Judge, upon him the said Reverend Edward Drax Free, unduly brought and afflicted ...' Particular attention was drawn to the partial prohibition that Free obtained from King's Bench in May 1826, and his subsequent appeal to the House of Lords, and to Nicholl continuing to proceed with the case on 3 June and 20 November 1826.
30 Ibid., pp. 14–15. The 'Inhibition and Citation' printed here provides a potted legal history of the case to 1 February 1827.

By the spring of 1827 the action between Burgoyne and Free was under scrutiny in the Court of Arches, where proceedings were suspended; in the House of Lords, where a judgement was still awaited; and the case was pending in the High Court of Delegates, which was itself waiting upon a decision from the Lords.[31] If this was not complicated enough, Addams was also by January 1827 indicating that he did not wish to act further as Dr Free's Proctor.[32]

March 1827 saw the beginnings of a further development: Dr Free appealed to the House of Lords against the rescinding by King's Bench of the costs he had been previously awarded and against the resumption of the case in the Court of Arches.[33] Judgement on the first matter did not arrive until June of that year, when the Lords' Committee scrutinising such appeals brought in a decision on the question of costs unfavourable to Free. Not only was the King's Bench rescission affirmed, but Free was ordered by the Lords to pay £100 to Burgoyne to cover costs newly incurred by opposing this appeal.[34]

Heartened by this but without doubt still clearly exasperated, Montagu Burgoyne renewed his petitioning of Parliament, addressing petitions to the Lords and Commons in June 1827 complaining about the immorality of Dr Free, and asking for a Bill enabling the Bishop to provide 'for Divine Worship in the Church 'till the Prosecution of the present Minister ... be concluded'.[35]

Although nothing came of this, Burgoyne would have been even more heartened by the House of Lords' eventual dismissal in June

---

31 *English Reports*, 162, pp. 921–27.

32 LPL, H427/55, p. 3.

33 *LJ*, 59, pp. 176, 227, 297, 336.

34 Ibid., pp. 376, 420, 437; *A Letter from Montagu Burgoyne, Esq., Churchwarden of Sutton, to his Brother Churchwardens, in the Diocese of Lincoln* (London, 1830), p. 23; *English Reports*, 4, pp. 1055–62, and 6, pp. 468–70, rehearse much of the legal history of the case down to 1828. The Lords went on for another year considering how to record this decision, *LJ*, 60, pp. 114, 148, 533, 580.

35 *LJ*, 59, p. 444; *Journal of the House of Commons* [hereafter *CJ*], 82, p. 607.

1828 of Free's appeal to it.[36] The High Court of Delegates, which had been waiting on this decision, was now able to assemble, and in July 1828 it dismissed Free's appeal to the Delegates, insisting that Sir John Nicholl had 'proceeded rightly, justly, and lawfully', and that the case in the Arches should be resumed.[37]

Things began to look black for Dr Free, particularly as Addams, his Proctor, renewed his request to be released from pleading the Rector's cause when business was resumed in the Arches in November.[38] Indeed, *The Times* reported that 'two proctors employed successively by Dr Free had declined proceeding any further for him'. The Judge refused to release Addams and the other Proctor, John George Crickitt, from their obligations, however, and proceeded to set in motion the machinery for summoning and examining witnesses.[39] Signs of Free's desperation can be discerned in his request in November 1828 to the President of St John's that the remainder of the sum promised him in 1809 from the Winterslow Fund should be remitted to him in London, 'as it is particularly wanted by return of post'. From the President's reply it is apparent that Free had some little time previously offered to resign from the Rectorship, perhaps in exchange for some College position. Seven years before this Free had proposed to the College a scheme for improving the stipend and conditions of service of the College Chaplain, seemingly to allow himself to accept the position. All such requests and offers were emphatically refused.[40]

Over the next few weeks a dozen witnesses nominated by Montagu Burgoyne were summoned to Doctors' Commons to be examined orally on the accusations contained in the Articles levelled against Free, so that court officers could draw up and submit to the court written depositions, signed by these same witnesses. In

36 *LJ*, 60, p. 580.
37 LPL, H427/51; Burgoyne, *A Letter ... to his Brother Churchwardens* (London, 1830), p. 23; *The Times*, 14 July 1828.
38 LPL, H427/55, p. 3; *The Times*, 4 November 1828, p. 3.
39 *The Times*, 12 November 1828, p. 4.
40 St John's College, MS L10 (v, vi).

the ecclesiastical courts all evidence submitted was written, a procedure that naturally dictated a slow rate of progress. The defendant, assisted by his Proctors, also drew up a series of questions – the 'Interrogatories' – which the witnesses were also obliged to answer.[41]

The whereabouts of some of these witnesses was obviously known. Indeed prior contacts had been established with Burgoyne or his Proctor in order to frame the Articles. This was the case with Maria Mackenzie. Burgoyne had arranged for her to swear affidavits in 1823 about her ill-treatment at the hands of Dr Free. When she deposed in 1828, she revealed that she had visited Doctors' Commons five times altogether: 'the first two times happened several years ago: both times she went to Mr Fox's office, and on one of such occasions met Mr Burgoyne there'.[42] Margaret and Mary Johnston were other witnesses with whom there had clearly been prior contact. Margaret Johnston deposed how Burgoyne had visited her when she worked for the Ricardos, about four years previously, and Mary Johnston was visited in her own home in Somers Town when Burgoyne came to look at the child she was fostering.[43]

Other witnesses were obviously more difficult to locate. Maria Crook may have been located through her family in Potton. By 1828 she had married her pedlar husband, changed her name and moved well away from her Bedfordshire birthplace. She deposed how the Churchwarden of Newport Pagnell sought her out and asked her if she was called Crook before her marriage to George

---

41 These witnesses were (in the order in which they deposed) Maria Mackenzie, William Hale, Thomas Siggins, Thomas Bainard Chappell, Catharine Raynes (formerly Siggins), John Hale, Margaret Johnston, Maria Roberts (formerly Crook), Mary Johnston, William Dennis, Mary (alias Eliza) Pierson, and the Reverend Peter Frazer. Dr Free appears to have played an active part in framing the Interrogatories: see LPL, H427/44, a somewhat disorganised list of questions, in his own hand, to be put to various witnesses. Maria Mackenzie made her statement on the Articles on 18 November, and returned to Doctors' Commons on 5 December to answer the Interrogatories.

42 LPL, H427/56, fos 8r, 10v–11r.

43 Ibid., fos 30v, 40r.

Roberts. When she acknowledged this, the Minister of Newport Pagnell came to see her, asking questions about her experiences with Free. He then told her that she had to travel to London to depose in the case.[44] Eliza Pierson also took some tracking down. An advertisement was placed in a London newspaper requesting her to contact a library in Crawford Street. From there she was directed to William Fox in Doctors' Commons.[45]

The whereabouts of the majority was well known, however, living as they did in or near Sutton. Because their examination would have involved them in troublesome journeying and expense, Burgoyne's Proctors sought and obtained permission from the court for two clerical commissioners to summon and examine nineteen other witnesses at Potton. These examinations on the subject of the Articles were carried out between 16 and 22 December 1828, and in the month following the witnesses responded to the Interrogatories put to them by Free and his Proctors.[46]

The resulting depositions have provided the evidential basis of the events described previously. Witness after witness attested to the truth of the facts assembled about Free's relationships with his housekeepers and the other abuses with which he was charged. His defence, particularly to the charges of sexual immorality, proved woefully inadequate. Character assassination and accusations of conspiracy were his principal weapons: the witnesses, he argued, were mostly immoral and dishonest individuals marshalled and schooled by Montagu Burgoyne, who was determined to bring him down for reasons of personal malice.

Thus Maria Crook was asked whether, when she lodged at the house of Nicholas Browne, the bricklayer of Potton, she had slept with him. She was also asked whether she had had a sexual relationship with James Teat, a carpenter of the same town. Maria denied both these implied accusations and denied also that she was already pregnant when she entered Free's service and that it was

44 Ibid., fos 36r and v.
45 Ibid., fol. 44v.
46 LPL, H427/19, 33, 36.

because of a quarrel with the Rector that she had sworn paternity of her child to him. In fact, her answers to some of these questions undoubtedly served to blacken Free's already murky image. She certainly broke some of the Rector's windows, she deposed, but this was a consequence of a quarrel, not the cause of one, and the quarrel itself arose over her refusal to take the pill that the Rector was so eager for her to take.[47]

Maria Mackenzie was subjected to a similar examination. She was asked whether, before entering the Rector's service, she was not already pregnant, having been 'picked up' by a man called Martin from the streets where she was 'plying the trade and business of a Prostitute'. As for her miscarriage, was this not the result of her poor health arising from a venereal infection picked up in the same fashion? After all it required only a kick from one of the Rector's lambs to bring it about, although admittedly the lamb was about to be castrated. She was also asked whether she had slept with a servant called Joseph Dennis during one of the Rector's temporary periods of absence.[48]

47 See above, p. 19. The Interrogatories put to Maria Roberts (née Crook) are in LPL, H427/43, and her deposition and answers are to be found in H427/56, fos 35r–38d.

48 The Interrogatories are in LPL, H427/37, and Maria's deposition (unfoliated) in H427/56. Free appears to have tried to blacken Maria Mackenzie's reputation on an earlier occasion. In the papers of William Howley, then Bishop of London, there exists the copy of an affidavit supposedly sworn by Ann Taylor, the Rector's housekeeper, before William Chapman of Biggleswade on 24 April 1826 and intended for the Court of King's Bench. In this affidavit Ann Taylor recalled conversations she allegedly had with Maria Mackenzie. When they were travelling once from Sutton to Biggleswade, in June or July 1823, Taylor said that she asked Mackenzie what good would come from exposing Free when all she would do would expose herself. To which Mackenzie reportedly replied, 'I don't care for that, as I have Mr Burgoyne on my side ... and I'll punish the Doctor ... if it costs me my life'. It was alleged that Mackenzie went on to report that Burgoyne had promised her £500 for her testimony, and that Mackenzie admitted that the Rector had in fact never touched her. On another occasion, journeying from Somers Town to Sutton, Mackenzie allegedly confessed that she was 'so ill that she should throw herself into the Hospital to get cured of all her diseases'.

Free also attempted to blacken Eliza Pierson's character, and in this case he appears to have been more successful, largely because of her refusal to answer several of the questions put to her. She declined to answer, for example, questions about how she had maintained herself before entering Free's service, how she had maintained herself subsequently, and who had provided money for the clothes in which she was currently attired, although she was prepared to depose that none of them had come Montagu Burgoyne.[49]

To say that the case thereafter moved easily and swiftly to a conclusion would be to varnish the truth. This could not be expected from preceding events. Dr Free continued, consciously or unconsciously, to exploit every opportunity for obstruction and delay. The court proved also to be remarkably indulgent to him, allowing him, for example, to bring in a 'Defensive Allegation' at the end of January 1829. This was devoted to a denial of the charges against him and a further derogation of the character of the witnesses. The document alleged that Free 'did not at any time form a criminal connection with them or either of them ... or took liberties with the person or solicited the chastity of the said Eliza Pierson' and 'that the said Maria Crook, Catharine Siggins, Margaret Johnston and Maria otherwise Mary Pierson [sic] were and are persons respectively of loose life and character, and of unchaste conduct and behaviour'. The document went on to allege that Maria Crook carried on a 'criminal connection and intercourse' with James Teat and William Brown; that Catharine Siggins did the same with one John Plowman, a farm servant of Biggleswade; that Johnston did likewise with a person or persons unknown; that Maria Mackenzie was involved with William Martin of Somers Town and later with

One could take this document more seriously if it were not in Dr Free's hand. See also note 57 below.

49 The Interrogatories are to be found in LPL, H427/43a; her deposition and answers in H427/56, fos 43r–46v. In his final review of the evidence, undertaken when sentencing Free, Sir John Nicholl stated that she was 'certainly not a woman of strict morality', *English Reports*, 162, p. 933.

Joseph Dennis. As for the indecent books, *Aristotle's Masterpiece* had accidently come into his possession and it might, equally accidently, have been seen by some of the witnesses, but he had never shown it to anyone. The document continued with rebuttals of the many charges levelled against him; it concluded with a further attack on all the ex-housekeepers, except Ann Taylor, who were characterised as 'persons of notoriously bad character ... who for gain or reward might easily be induced or prevailed upon to swear falsely'.[50]

No witnesses, however, were produced by Dr Free in support of his arguments, and the submission drew rebuttals from Burgoyne's Proctors.[51] By now the proceedings had stretched into May 1829, at which point Dr Free appeared and swore to the court that his finances were exhausted, and this was why he was unable to examine any witnesses to prove the contents of his Defensive Allegation. He also swore that he had been confined to his bed through illness, totally unable to travel to London, and that just before the next scheduled session of the court he had received a letter from Addams, his Proctor, running thus:

> Rev'd Sir, You will recollect that Monday next is the first day of term and as I proceed no further for you, you should appoint another proctor or attend yourself for the care of your cause.[52]

Because of all this, he pleaded for, and was given, until the next court day to bring in the 'Exceptive Allegation' that he was permitted to enter.[53] Partly because by now he had no Proctor, Free

---

50 LPL, H427/20 (28 January 1829).
51 Ibid., H427/46, where Fox states, for example, that Crook, Siggins, Johnston, Mackenzie and Pierson far from being 'Persons of notoriously bad Character ... were and are respectively Persons of good Character and Reputation'.
52 LPL, H427/47.
53 The rules relating to Exceptive Allegations were strict. *The Report of the 1832 Royal Commission on the Ecclesiastical Courts* stated (*Parliamentary Papers* [hereafter *PP*], 1831–32, 24, p. 2) that 'The Examination and Cross-examination of Witnesses is kept secret until Publication passes, after which either party is allowed to except to the credit of any witness,

was given time to prepare these submissions, though Sir John Nicholl's patience was clearly being sorely stretched by the Rector's persistent obstruction of the case. He had had abundant time, said Nicholl, 'to vindicate his character; instead of which he had been exerting himself to hang up the cause in this court by instituting proceedings in other courts'.[54]

The Rector did eventually bring in his Exceptive Allegation on 29 May 1829, and Free used the occasion to address the court 'in a speech full of invective and irrelevant observations'. He complained that 'he was persecuted by his opponents because he had prayed for the late Queen, which he did from religious, not political motives'. Sir John Nicholl refused to accept Free's Exceptive Allegation on the grounds that it was procedurally too late and was offered in too irregular a form. He advised that the case was concluded and that he would at the start of the following term give his sentence. He also advised Free that he should attend on that occasion. The Rector reportedly replied that given the way he had been treated there was little point in his attending further, to which Nicholl apparently responded, 'You can do as you please in that respect, Sir'.[55]

So, in mid June 1829, the case at last came to sentence, and Dr Free, despite his threat to attend no further, seated himself in the First Advocate's chair, to the left of Sir John Nicholl, continually interrupting the proceedings.

Stephen Lushington summed up the case of the promoter, Montagu Burgoyne, pointing out that various women had sworn on

upon matter contained in his deposition. The exception must be confined to such matter, and not made to general character, for that must be pleaded before publication; nor can the exception refer to matter before pleaded, for that should be contradicted also before publication. The exception must also tend to show that the Witness had deposed falsely and corruptly.' See also Richard Burn, *The Ecclesiastical Law* (9th edn, London 1842), iii, p. 312.

54 *The Times*, 21 May 1829, p. 3.
55 LPL, H427/48, appears to be the basis of the Exceptive Allegation. See also *The Times*, 30 May 1829, p. 6, and *English Reports*, 162, pp. 929–31.

oath that Free was the father of their children, and that the Rector had indeed paid for their support. If these were women of unchaste life and conduct, as had been argued, what was a clergyman doing keeping them in his service? As for the indecent books, it was the duty of a clergyman to destroy such books or to prevent them coming into the sight of servants. Whilst there was no evidence that the Rector was an habitual drunkard, said Lushington, it was sufficiently proved that he indulged in drink and improper language. It was amply proved also that he had converted the churchyard into a farmyard, that he had sold the lead off the chancel roof for his own profit, and that he had threatened with a horsewhip a Churchwarden who had asked to hold a vestry in the chancel. Lushington concluded with a defence of the motives of Montagu Burgoyne, who had acted not out of malice but out of a laudable sense of public duty.[56]

Dr Free conducted his own defence. He began by attempting at this late stage to introduce affidavits in support of his character and conduct. One came, he said, from William Bunting, the Parish Clerk.[57] The other came, said Free, 'from a practitioner of great eminence, and therefore it was unnecessary to name him'. The latter allegedly said of the judgement of the Court of Arches in admitting the Articles against Free that it was 'the most miserable jargon ever pronounced by a judge'. The Rector then renewed his attacks on his former housekeepers, claimed that he had kept his 'anatomical books' under lock and key, and that he was well known to be an enemy of strong drink. Indeed, 'many persons who had known him for twenty years as a Fellow of a College could testify

---

56 On Lushington see S. M. Waddams, *Law, Politics and the Church of England: The Career of Stephen Lushington, 1782–1873* (Cambridge, 1982).

57 There exists in Bishop Howley's papers another affidavit intended seemingly for the Court of King's Bench, 'expressive of the false charges made against the Rector of Sutton'. It was supposedly sworn by William Bunting before William Chapman of Biggleswade on 20 May 1826, but the copy is in Dr Free's hand. In the affidavit Bunting swears that Free is totally undeserving of the charges laid against him in the Court of Arches, LPL, Fulham Papers (Howley), 16, fos 210–11.

that he was the most temperate man there'. He also raged against Montagu Burgoyne and other members of that family. He claimed, it was the combination of age, gout and the treatment he had received from the Burgoynes that was responsible for his propensity to stagger, inducing false beliefs that he was drunk. Free concluded his extraordinary performance by declaring his intention to publish in due course a short work entitled *Burgoyniana, or Anecdotes of the Burgoyne Family*.

Sir John Nicholl, who had several times admonished Free, proceeded himself to review the case and to pronounce sentence. It was, he said, a painful case, painful for Free and painful for the church to which he belonged, though as he pointed out very few such cases surfaced amongst the thousands of clergymen attached to that body. The business had been costly and had lasted a long time, but this was not the fault of his court; it might have been concluded in 1825 had Free not taken every opportunity of 'obstructing and impeding' the proceedings. Nicholl related the various steps taken by the Rector to delay his prosecution, before moving to a detailed review of the evidence presented to his court. He did not dwell, related the *Morning Advertiser*, on the 'disgusting profligate history' of the defendant, but he drew attention to the illegitimate children that Free was maintaining – 'thus shamefully converting his rectory-house into a common brothel'. 'Slight deviations in morality from the infirmity of human nature may be punished by admonition', said the Judge, 'but after this history has gone forth no hope must be entertained that the respect can be restored which ought to exist betwixt parishioners and their clergyman.' It was his painful duty to pronounce the Articles sufficiently proved to decree that Dr Free should be deprived of the living of Sutton and be liable for the costs of the case.[58]

A week later Dr Free appealed to the High Court of Delegates against the verdict, claiming that the Judge, Sir John Nicholl, showed

58 See *The Times*, 16 June 1829, p. 3; *Morning Advertiser*, 16 June 1829, p. 3; *English Reports*, 162, pp. 931–35; a copy of the sentence itself is in LA, FB4, fos 342–43.

undue partiality to Burgoyne.[59] The Earl of Hardwicke deplored in the House of Lords the fact that this appeal meant that Dr Free could still continue to operate as Rector of Sutton, and Lord Lyndhurst, the Lord Chancellor, promised that he would do all in his power to bring forward the appeal hearing.[60]

The Delegates, when eventually they set to work in 1830, reviewed the evidence all over again, listening in the process to Burgoyne's Proctors and to Dr Free. They considered and rejected various arguments, such as that deprivation of a living was too severe a punishment for sexual misbehaviour that fell short of adultery, and that a clergyman could not be deprived for fornication without having previously been warned of such misbehaviour. There was no limit to the Rector's resourcefulness, but it was to no avail: the Delegates on 15 February 1830 upheld the sentence pronounced in the Arches, and Dr Free was deprived of his living.[61]

Remembering that formal complaints were laid before the Archdeacon of Bedford in October 1823 and that the rejection by the High Court of Delegates of Dr Free's final appeal did not come until February 1830, it might be said that it took over six years to deprive the Rector of his living. Even if we confine attention to his prosecution in the Court of Arches, the business seems an extraordinarily protracted one. The case began there in October 1824 and it was not concluded until June 1829, four years and eight months later. Why did it take so long to unseat the Rector of Sutton?

Delay characterised the prosecution right from the outset. The ecclesiastical authorities appeared to be uncertain as to where he should be prosecuted, and indeed whether he should be prosecuted, an uncertainty that was a compound of ignorance, fear of expense and perhaps internal tension amongst senior officials within the diocese of Lincoln. We have noted how William Fox had to ask Charles Bailey, the Registrar at Bedford, whether the Archdeacon

59 LPL, H427/49; *The Times*, 24 June 1829, p. 3.
60 *Huntingdon, Bedford and Peterborough Gazette*, 27 June 1829, p. 4.
61 *The Times*, 16 February 1830, p. 4; *English Reports*, 162, p. 991.

of Bedford had the authority to conduct a prosecution leading to deprivation, and how Fox offered the suggestion that the suit should be brought in the Bishop of Lincoln's court. The Bishop of Lincoln was fearful, however, of the costs involved, particularly once Lushington and Fox had alerted him to their view that the principal charges of incontinency could not be pressed because the offences were deemed out of term by the Act of 1787. Although the decision was eventually made to start the process of prosecution, and to do so in the court of Richard Smith, the Bishop's Commissary of the Archdeaconry of Bedford, that decision provoked a protest from the Chancellor of the diocese, Dr Battine, who considered that his diocesan court at Lincoln had been by-passed. Although this protest was overruled, it effectively delayed procedings in the Court of Arches for nearly three months between November 1824 and January 1825.

Even if there had been no such delay, speedy progress was not to be expected in the Court of Arches. There were not very many court sessions in the course of a year, as Sir John Nicholl explained to the Ecclesiastical Court Commissioners: 'There are four Terms in each year, and four regular Sessions in each Term.'[62] The total reliance upon written evidence was not conducive to speed and, even when prosecutions were underway, the elaborate sequence of manuscript Articles, Interrogatories and Allegations from both sides meant that the case proceeded like some stately legal quadrille from one court session to the next. Pressed by the Commissioners in 1830, Dr Dodson, an Advocate in Doctors' Commons, was forced to admit that 'In the present mode of proceeding ... a very considerable degree of expense and delay is incurred', though he argued that this was principally due to the way in which characters like Dr Free obstructed justice by appealing at every opportunity and applying for prohibitions against the ecclesiastical court proceeding with the prosecution. Indeed, he argued, once the Court of Arches was at liberty to press its case against Sutton's Rector it proceeded

62 *PP*, 1831–32, part 2, p. 261.

to a conclusion in less than twelve months.[63] Dr Phillimore, another Advocate in Doctors' Commons, made the same point. Asked whether 'The efficient proceedings in the late case referred to, of Dr Free, did not continue long in court?', he replied, 'Not in the Ecclesiastical Court; the principal delay arose from the removal to the Courts of Common Law'.[64]

There was clearly considerable truth in Phillimore's argument. The existence of separate systems of law – ecclesiastical and secular – and the enduring tensions between them were very effectively exploited by Dr Free.[65] His appeal to King's Bench in May 1825 took a year to be resolved, the action in the Arches being meanwhile suspended. The appeal to the House of Lords in May 1826 was not resolved until June 1828; this delayed proceedings for only another half a year, because Nicholl resumed the Arches prosecution in November 1826.

This in turn led to Free's first appeal to the High Court of Delegates in November 1826, an appeal that was not dismissed until July 1828. His second appeal to the Delegates in June 1829 was resolved more speedily, but it still took over six months to arrive. Appeals to the Delegates almost always took time to be resolved. The Court was a mixed body consisting of three or four judges from the principal courts of Common Law and between three and five Civilians, and one at least of the Common Law judges had to be present. Matters invariably had to wait until they were free of other responsibilities and thus able to sit in on the appeal.

Finally, in looking for reasons why cases such as these took such time, we should not discount the determination of the ecclesiastical authorities to be fair, giving accused clerics every opportunity to defend themselves and to appeal against possible injustices. When Phillimore was asked by the Ecclesiastical Court Commissioners in 1830 to offer an opinion on such prosecutions he responded by saying:

63 Ibid., appendix A, p. 168.
64 Ibid., p. 162.
65 These tensions are further explored in Chapter 7 below.

I am very sensible something is wanting in that respect; the forms of the process at present enable persons to extend the proceedings to a great length, but that arises from the nature of the suit, which is a criminal suit, and from the reluctance the law has to hold any person concluded by a criminal charge without allowing to the party accused the utmost latitude of defence.[66]

Dr Free was certainly offered every opportunity to mount a defence, as well as to appeal against decisions made. In the end, however, even his resourcefulness ran dry and in February 1830 the sentence of deprivation was finally confirmed.

66   *PP*, 1831–32, appendix A, p. 162.

6

End Game

'THE SENTENCE OF DEPRIVATION pronounced by the Court of Arches was confirmed by the Court of Delegates on the 11th of February', relates Montagu Burgoyne's *Letter ... to his Brother Churchwardens* of 1830, 'and on the 12 March I received Orders of Sequestration, directing me to take possession of the Rectory, and all things appertaining thereunto, together with the Iron Chest, Register, Communion Plate, and all Property belonging to the Church.'[1] Obtaining such powers was one thing; enforcing them was quite another. Prising Dr Free out of the Rectory proved, perhaps utterly predictably, to be a difficult task.

Burgoyne organised a reading on 22 March in the parish church of the notices of the Rector's deprivation and the sequestration, before a congregation 'more numerous I think than I ever remember to have been assembled in Sutton'. A Mr Yates read, at Burgoyne's invitation, the Morning Service and preached a sermon. The latter was based on Matthew 20, the parable of the workers in the vineyard cheated by their employer, and it obviously struck home: 'The discourse', wrote Burgoyne, 'commanded ... their attention.' The day before this, however, he had reported to the Bishop of Lincoln that Dr Free had declared that he would not move, despite, or

---

1 Burgoyne, *A Letter from Montagu Burgoyne, Esq., Churchwarden of Sutton, to his Brother Churchwardens* (London, 1830) [hereafter Burgoyne, *A Letter to his Brother Churchwardens* (1830)], p. 3. In fact the sentence of deprivation was confirmed by the Delegates on 15 February 1830, ibid., p. 26.

because of, the fact that he 'has sold every thing what belonged to him and what did not'. Burgoyne pleaded for the Archdeacon to visit the parish.[2]

That official, Dr Bonney, quickly complied, and within the week he was relating to the Bishop the results of his visit. He met Montagu Burgoyne in Potton on the 23 March where, the latter reported, 'Dr Free ... was fortified in the Rectory House, and barred the door against any person connected with him as Sequestrator'. Burgoyne had, however, turned out of office Free's Parish Clerk, supposedly for being drunk on the the day before Sacrament Sunday, forcibly having him removed from the seat in which he customarily sat, an action that the Archdeacon informed him greatly exceeded his powers as Churchwarden.[3] On the following day, the Archdeacon travelled to Sutton where Burgoyne invited him to inspect the Rectory, but, as Bonney reported, 'Every gate from the Church yard was firmly fastened'. The two of them, accompanied by the new Curate, Mr Whittingham, 'went round to the principal entrance, rang the Bell at a small door, and from a larger Gate appeared a maid Servant'. She, almost certainly the immensely loyal Ann Taylor, informed the Archdeacon that the Rector was prepared to see him, but was not willing to see Burgoyne. The Archdeacon alone then entered the house which, he reported, was almost bereft of furniture, a sale apparently having taken place some days earlier. Dr Free appeared and accompanied him upstairs, complaining all the while about the way in which witnesses had perjured themselves against him, and the treatment meted out to his Clerk by Montagu Burgoyne. Bonney reported that he listened patiently to this torrent of complaint and then discreetly left. Outside the Rectory he encountered a carpenter waiting for word that he and other workmen could enter the house to begin refurbishing it, but the Archdeacon warned him that 'no violence might be used, not even

---

2   LA, COR B5/7/2/11–13.
3   Although the name of the Clerk was not given, it was probably William Bunting.

A

LETTER

FROM

MONTAGU BURGOYNE, ESQ.

CHURCHWARDEN OF SUTTON,

TO

HIS BROTHER CHURCHWARDENS,

IN THE

Diocese of Lincoln;

GIVING

A SUMMARY ACCOUNT,

OF

THE PROSECUTION, CONVICTION, AND DEPRIVATION

OF THE

REV. DR. EDWARD DRAX FREE,

RECTOR OF SUTTON,

IN THE COUNTY OF BEDFORD;

WITH A FEW

USEFUL HINTS

ON THE SERIOUSNESS OF THE OATH TAKEN BY CHURCHWARDENS,
AND THE IMPORTANCE OF THEIR DUTIES.

———

The above Sentence of Deprivation was passed by the Court of Arches, and confirmed
by the House of Lords and the High Court of Delegates.

———

LONDON:

PUBLISHED BY RIVINGTONS, ST. PAUL'S CHURCH-YARD,
AND WATERLOO-PLACE, PALL-MALL; AND J. HATCHARD, PICCADILLY.

———

1830.

Price One Shilling.

8. Title page of *A Letter from Montagu Burgoyne, Esq.,
Churchwarden of Sutton, to his Brother Churchwardens* (1830).

the lifting of a latch'. 'I suppose', reported Bonney to the Bishop, 'they expected I should order them to carry the Rectory by Storm.'[4]

In the event the Rectory was not taken until 11 April and then it was acquired, as Burgoyne reported, 'not by *force* but, by *stratagem*':

> The Sequestrator perceiving the obstinacy of the deprived Rector, and dreading the commission of murder, which he and the young woman living with him threatened to several persons, showing pistols, and once pulling a trigger, felt himself justified in blockading the house without using any force; permitting the Inhabitants to go out, but none to enter.

'Thus', Burgoyne's second pamphlet explains, 'the inhabitants were excluded from all provisions', and, it continues, 'This they endured for ten days, when this unhappy man was compelled by hunger to quit the house'. His account published in 1830 tells us:

> After his departure, the Sequestrator gave orders to the Constables to demand, *three times*, the Register and the Church property; but no answer being received, that part of the house which was locked up was broken open, the Register and Church Property taken and deposited in the Church, and the young woman, without any violence, ejected from the house, which is now in the possession of the Sequestrator, in trust for the next Incumbent.

Dr Free fled first to nearby Potton, from where, Burgoyne tells us, 'he proceeded on foot to London, as no person would assist him with any other conveyance'.[5] Despite the previously mentioned sale, he left behind in the Rectory possessions to the value of £100 or more, and St John's College took opinion of counsel as to whether these could be retained to offset the cost of dilapidations. This Mr Hudson, the Surveyor, had set, before Free's exit from the house, at £285 3s. od., but Free's successor later put the figure

4 LA, COR B5/7/2/14.
5 Burgoyne, *A Letter to his Brother Churchwardens* (1830), p. 4, and *A Letter to the Churchwardens of the Diocese of Lincoln* (London, 1831), pp. 4–5.

A

LETTER

TO THE

CHURCHWARDENS OF THE DIOCESE OF LINCOLN,

BY

MONTAGU BURGOYNE, ESQ.

WITH REFERENCE TO A LETTER ADDRESSED TO THEM LAST YEAR
ON THE SUBJECT OF THE

PROSECUTION AND CONVICTION

OF

DR. FREE,

LATE RECTOR OF SUTTON, IN THE COUNTY OF BEDFORD.

IN THE LETTER NOW ADDRESSED TO THEM, HIS REASONS ARE GIVEN FOR DECLINING
THE CHURCHWARDENSHIP, THOUGH REQUESTED BY THE RECTOR
TO ACT IN THAT CAPACITY.

IN THIS PUBLICATION IS INSERTED

A FAC SIMILE OF A LETTER ADDRESSED TO SIR JOHN BURGOYNE
BY OLIVER CROMWELL, IN THE YEAR 1648.

The present Publication will be presented *gratis* to Churchwardens ; to all other
persons the price will be One Shilling. The Profits (if any) will be applied to the
Support of a School of Industry at Potton, and the encouragement of Allotments of
Land provided for the Labouring Poor in Beds, and the two contiguous Counties of
Huntingdon and Cambridge.

LONDON:

Printed by Shaw and Sons, 137, Fetter Lane ;

AND SOLD BY RIVINGTONS, ST. PAUL'S CHURCH-YARD AND WATERLOO-PLACE ;
RIDGWAY, PICCADILLY ;
WEBB, BEDS. ; AND OTHER COUNTRY BOOKSELLERS.

1831.

Price One Shilling.

9. Title page of *A Letter to the Churchwardens of the Diocese of Lincoln* (1831).

at between £400 and £500. Stephen Lushington's legal advice was cautious. He thought that the College could not take possession of Free's goods as part payment for dilapidations, but that as 'a matter of prudence though not of Law' they, or the new Rector, should hang on to them to facilitate a settlement of some kind with Dr Free.[6]

Meanwhile St John's College set their mind to the succession. In April 1830 they granted £150 towards the cost of repairing the Rectory, and in July they nominated Charles Dethicke Blythe as the next incumbent. Within months of his nomination Blythe married, no doubt to the College's great relief.[7]

Dr Free, cast adrift without permanent residence or regular stipend, becomes a shadowy figure. He appears to have moved from one lodging to another in London. In 1832 we find him writing from Hardwicke Street, Clerkenwell; a petition of November 1835 gives his address as '22 Trinity Street, Borough' (presumably Southwark); whilst letters of July 1839 were addressed from 'Mr Gibbon's Chambers, 3 Pump Court, Temple'. We know this because he emerged periodically from the shadows to haunt a succession of individuals and institutions. He employed a solicitor in September 1832 to enquire of the Bishop of Lincoln why he had been refused the £62 10s. od. due, he claimed, for the Lady Day quarter of 1830. The Bishop's Secretary, John Burder, also acknowledged that Dr Free had called upon him several times 'upon this and other Matters of an appeal respecting his College'.[8]

This is the first reference we have to Dr Free's ingenious solution to his new financial difficulties: he would seek readmission to his Fellowship at St John's. To this end, he began soliciting support from old Oxford acquaintances. One such was Dr Philip Bliss,

---

6 St John's College, MS L10 (viii, x). Burgoyne's 1831 pamphlet tells us that 'He left furniture to the amount of £230, which the new Rector is willing to take, and give him a receipt for all dilapidations, which have been valued at £400', *A Letter to the Churchwardens of the Diocese of Lincoln* (1831), p. 5.

7 St John's College, Register, viii, 1795–1834, pp. 418, 422, 429.

8 LA, Cor B5/7/2/17–18.

Keeper of the University Archives, from whom he received the following reply:

> Dear Sir,
>
> I received your Parcel, and would willingly do you any service in my power, from having known you as a member of St John's, although subsequent events have rendered it impossible for me to have any further intercourse or correspondence with you.
>
> I return your Papers and have enclosed a Sovereign which is all it is in my power to offer you.
>
> Having quitted St John's College for several years, I have no influence with any of its members.[9]

The College must have been equally unreceptive to his proposals, for the next evidence of his operations that we have is a petition from Free, drawn up in Doctors' Commons in 1832, addressed to the Bishop of Winchester, the College Visitor. This pleaded for his reinstatement as Senior Fellow on a number of grounds. One claim was that he had tried to decline Sutton after the living was offered to him in favour of another parish, but that the College refused to present him to it. Another was that it had reneged on a promise of £200 for repair of the Rectory, only giving him £50 for this purpose 'though he repeatedly wrote for the remainder'.[10] This was coupled with the plea that he had erected various buildings at

---

9 BL, MS Add., 34571, fos 145, 152.

10 The College's minute for 17 October 1808 reads: 'It was agreed that a Sum not exceeding Fifty Pounds be granted from the Winterslow Fund to the Living of Sutton in Bedfordshire to enable the Rector to floor a Parlour which is at present laid with brick', St John's College, Register, viii, 1795–1834, p. 154. A later entry, made in October 1833, reads 'At a Meeting of the President and Ten Seniors: A Claim having been Made on the Part of Dr Free, formerly a Fellow of the College, for the Sum of one hundred and fifty pounds granted to the Rector of Sutton in Bedfordshire by order of Convocation on the 23rd of November 1809, Which order, the condition of the grant not having been complied with, was rescinded on the 6th of February 1813; it was agreed that the Society do deny the validity of such claim, and refuse to accede thereto', ibid., viii, p. 470.

Sutton and 'had defended the College boundaries by extensive suits' against the rapacious Burgoynes. A further claim, one that was to occupy him for years to come, was that his Fellowship should be restored because he had not 'at any time given a written resignation which the statutes require'. All this was coupled with pleas of hardship, such as

> that your petitioner is now in his sixty-eighth year of his age, without a dwelling and without support, and not able to save anything though he has received near three hundred pounds per annum, owing to the litigious disposition of the Burgoyne family; his late protracted defence having not only cost him near £1200, but likewise various other concomitant expences owing to the extrajudicial proceedings ...[11]

The Bishop was apparently unmoved by these pleas, for 1833 saw Dr Free seeking a writ from the Court of King's Bench to compel the Visitor to admit him as as a Fellow of St John's.[12] The College was forced to defend its position, the President sending to London copies of the statutes relating to the relinquishing of Fellowships, as well as his own affidavit swearing that Dr Free's name had long been omitted from the College's books. He regretted that the Bishop should have 'so much trouble on this subject of so worthless an individual and in a case apparently so easy'.[13] Nothing connected with Dr Free, however, was ever easy.

In September 1833 he renewed his appeal to the Bishop, striking at the outset a note far from diplomatic with the statement that 'the said Right Reverend Father Dr Sumner does not appear to have treated the [previous] appeal with that solemnity and reciprocal feeling' that the founder's statutes merited.[14]

---

11 HRO, 21 M 65 / J7.
12 *The Times*, 8 May 1833, p. 3; 9 May 1833, p. 6. The Court of King's Bench, Free reported in 1839, accepted the College's argument that he had ceased to be a Fellow, and that the Bishop had, therefore, no jurisdiction to settle the matter, *The Times*, 26 January 1839, p. 7.
13 HRO, 21 M65/J7, letter of 29 May 1833.
14 Ibid., petition of 11 September 1833.

In October 1833 Dr Free visited Oxford and went to St John's, where he took breakfast in the Common Room before requesting an interview with the President. The latter declined to see him, however, and ordered the College Porter to see him off the premises. Free believed 'that if he had not left the College peaceable he would have been driven out by force'.[15]

Two years later he was still pursuing the Bishop of Winchester in King's Bench, whilst also vigorously petitioning him to visit the College on his behalf.[16] His case for reinstatement at St John's was now based on his own, highly personal interpretation of the College statutes, and the denial that his acceptance of a College living had extinguished his Fellowship. Free's appeal to the Bishop elicited the response from the President of St John's that 'The Document itself is of so vague a character that it is difficult to arrange my observations upon it'.[17] Free apparently met the Bishop in London in May 1836, after which he was informed that his petition could not be granted, though the Bishop allegedly stated a willingness to consider any further arguments that Free might adduce. This was a great mistake.[18]

Petition after petition was hereafter pressed upon the long-suffering Sumner, as Free's cries of penury became ever more intense. The Bishop could not allow him as a Senior Fellow, he argued in September 1835, 'to languish on a precarious subsistence for two or three years, and pledge every thing, even his paraphernalia and his library, the gift of his Literary Friends'.[19] His petition of May 1836 pointed out that he was

> now in his 73rd year and has no means of subsistence, that
> he is reduced to the most miserable poverty, and now in

---

15 Ibid., reported in his petition of 21 May 1836.
16 *The Times*, 2 February 1835, p. 3; HRO, 21 M65/J7, petitions of 10 February 1835 and 4 November 1835.
17 HRO, M65/J7, letter of 21 April 1835.
18 This meeting is reported in Free's petition of 27 July 1838, HRO, M65/J7.
19 Ibid., 7 September 1835.

his old age deprived of all those comforts he has been used to from his youth upwards, that he is emaciated in body for want of necessary food and raiment, [and] that he has hitherto been most providentially preserved alive by casual donations . . .[20]

His state was such, implied a letter of 1837, that for the Bishop to continue to ignore it would 'be a stain upon your character and indelible blot as a dereliction of duty'. Free also announced his intention 'as Senior Fellow' to receive the sacrament in St John's College Chapel on the forthcoming Christmas Day, warning the Bishop that if he met with any obstruction he would hold him personally responsible.[21] Free already had experience of being hustled out of College: this had happened, as we have noted, when he had demanded to see the President in 1833. In June 1837 he entered St John's 'habited as a Fellow' and, he alleged, was assaulted by one of the Porters and forced to leave the College.[22]

In 1838 he began another action in King's Bench against the Bishop, an action that did not conclude until 1839. This time he sought a writ compelling the Bishop to visit St John's in order to adjudicate on his petition of 1837, a petition which argued that he was as an ex-Fellow entitled, at the very least, to support out of the endowments of the College, with arrears dating back to the time of his deprivation in 1830. His case could not have been helped by his reading of a protest against a former King's Bench decision announced by Lord Denman in 1833 that had gone against him. He recounted how he had 'impeached the conduct of Lord Denman to the King and to Lord John Russell, and also made a communication to the Lord Chancellor', but he had received no satisfaction from any of them. The court decided, not surprisingly, that this latest application of Free's, despite being for 'sustenance only', was not very different in substance from his earlier ones and

20 Ibid., 21 May 1836.
21 Ibid., letter of 22 December 1837.
22 Reported in the petition of 27 July 1838.

rejected it. Dr Free responded furiously: 'Am I, then, a Minister of Christ, to be doomed to beg my bread throughout the country?' He threatened this time to write to the Prime Minister, and to the Queen 'who has probably more kindness of feeling than the bishop'. The latter, he continued, has three palaces', whilst 'I have no bed to lie on, and have been for three days together without food, at the age of 76'.[23]

This appears to have represented Free's last attempt at using the courts to escape his predicament. Thereafter he was reduced once more to direct appeals to the College to rescue him. He wrote directly to the President and Senior Fellows of St John's in June 1839, applying for restoration to the rights and privileges of a Fellow 'agreeable to the precepts of Christianity', but also, perhaps somewhat optimistically, laying claim to the presentation of the Rectory of Tackley, Oxfordshire, 'as it is my wish and intention not to reside in college, nor to interfere with the discipline of the same during the few years Providence may allow me to remain'.[24] Characteristically, a letter to the Bishop of Winchester followed, entering a *caveat* against any other Fellow being presented to that living, and reminding the Visitor that Free expected him to 'act with that Christian Benevolence which you have so solemnly pledged yourself to practise and forward'.[25]

One mystery is how Dr Free managed to sustain the litigation that began soon after his arrival in Sutton, and the continual barrage of petitioning and litigation that followed his deprivation in 1830. Actions at the Bedford Assizes and Quarter Sessions must have cost him a pretty sum even before he began to defend himself in the ecclesiastical courts. He calculated his income in 1821 at over £400 a year, and whilst he may have been able to save something from this in the years of his incumbency, we must remember that by May 1829 he was pleading that his finances were exhausted by the

23 This King's Bench case is reported fully in *The Times*, 28 January 1839, p. 7.
24 HRO, 21 M65/J7, 29 June 1839.
25 Ibid., 4 July 1839.

defence of his cause in the Court of Arches.[26] Indeed a month later, in June 1829, he was arrested by the Sheriff of Middlesex and incarcerated for several months in the King's Bench Prison for a debt of £821 owing to his long-time Common Law attorney, Faithful Croft.[27] Consequently the Bishop of Lincoln not only picked up the bill for Free's prosecution in the Court of Arches but also, as Burgoyne related, 'a great part of that which attached to the Defendant, who declared himself unable to pay'.[28] The Ecclesiastical Court Commissioners later reported that 'the expenses incurred by successive Diocesans, in prosecuting the Suit, amounted to a sum of not less than £1500'.[29] Nevertheless, considerable amounts must have been dissipated by Free himself in law suits, and after 1830 he had, of course, no stipend to sustain him. He confessed in 1839 that he had spent the very substantial sum of £2000 upon litigation, a not improbable figure given the frequency with which he went to law and his propensity to lose cases.[30]

But where did the money come from, particularly after 1830? Some probably did come from the liquidation of whatever assets he possessed, as Free several times claimed. His campaigns may also have been occasionally supported by others, for motives that can only be guessed at. Sir John Campbell declared a willingness to act for him in King's Bench in 1835, apparently because Free had no attorney and Campbell professed his willingness to 'do the same for any of his Majesty's subjects when they had not the means of obtaining professional assistance'.[31] Free claimed in 1839 that he would have died of want 'if it had not been for the charity of an archbishop, a noble duke, and some members of the bar'. What truth there was in this assertion we do not know, but it is interesting that, when he railed against the King's Bench Justices on that

26 See above, Chapter 5, p. 39.
27 PRO, King's Bench Prison Commitment Book, Pris 4/40, p. 167; St John's College, MS L10 (vii).
28 Burgoyne, *A Letter to his Brother Churchwardens* (1830), p. 5.
29 *PP*, 1831–32, 24, 1, Report, p. 56.
30 *The Times*, 28 January 1839, p. 7.
31 Ibid., 2 February 1835, p. 3.

occasion, Free noted that 'Lord Denman ... who was formerly his advocate and with whom he had repeatedly taken counsel, professed great kindness towards him ...'[32]

Although costs were frequently awarded against him, as they were in his unsuccessful King's Bench suit in 1839, there was as the Bishop of Winchester realised on that occasion 'not the slightest probability of a Shilling being received from him'. Others consequently picked up the bills: in this case St John's College paid the Bishop's legal expenses, as they did also in 1836.[33]

It does seem likely that Dr Free survived after 1830 largely on charity. Writing to the President of St John's in January 1841, William Stone, the Rector of Christ Church, Spitalfields, provided a vivid picture of him in these years:

> You are probably aware, that, for many years past, he has been about London, during which time he has been indebted for a miserable and precarious subsistence to the charity of some of its respectable Lay inhabitants, and the occasional reluctant contribution of the Clergy. As one of the latter body, I was myself visited by him some years ago, but, knowing no more of him than what I had collected from the public Prints during my residence at Oxford, I declined having any Communication with him, and, in the first instance, refused him any pecuniary assistance. After that, however, I saw him so destitute of all the necessaries of life, that I could no longer withold my Compassion; and, ever since, I have felt myself compelled to listen to his application, and to give him occasional relief in food and money. His visits to me have, of late, become more frequent, and from this circumstance, added to observations which have dropped from him and his deplorable personal appearance, I suspect that he has nearly exhausted the charity of his old contributors, and that, at Seventy-Seven Years of age, he must either starve, or obtrude this revolting case of

32 Ibid., 28 January 1839, p. 7.
33 St John's College, MS L10 (xi).

Clerical wretchedness upon the respectable Members of the Community.

Stone went on to assume that 'the Society of St John's must feel most painfully the degraded position of this outcast member' and to ask whether the College could do anything for him. He also recounted, however, a recent conversation in which Free intimated that he intended 'to prosecute measures for his restoration to his Fellowship', but that if help was forthcoming from St John's 'he might be prevailed upon to give no further trouble, and to withdraw himself from public observation'![34]

President Wynter's reply was distinctly frosty. 'Dr Free', he wrote, 'has no claim whatever upon the sympathy or consideration of any Individual of our Body.' As his draft reply continued, 'Whilst a member of it, he was, I am told, a nuisance to every one belonging to it'. He became, moreover, 'an indelible disgrace' to the society. Any attempt by the College to relieve his misery, he warned, would be interpreted as an indirect acknowledgment of his right to be restored to his Fellowship. As an example of this he related how some years previously he, and four or five others, organised privately a life pension of £20 a year for Free. This was to be handed over to a friend of the ex-Rector, an attorney, on condition that Free would never know where the money came from. Unfortunately, the attorney broke the agreement and Free at once claimed it 'as an allowance granted to him by the College in consideration of his renouncing his pretended rights'. The College would not respond to his threats of prosecution by 'buying him off'. He could, of course, put the College to trouble and expense 'as he has obviously done by his Attacks upon our Visitor, whose charges at Law we could not do otherwise than to pay', but the College had a duty to itself and similar institutions in both universities not to recognise as a Fellow someone who had ceased to be one for more than thirty years.[35]

---

34 St John's College, MS L10 (xii).
35 Ibid.

Free may have been emotionally, though not financially, sustained by the death in March 1836, at the age of eighty-five, of his old foe Montagu Burgoyne, who had pursued the Rector right through to the deprivation of his living and had engineered his removal from Sutton. He was present for example in the Court of Arches in June 1829 when Sir John Nicholl pronounced sentence. An outburst of laughter from Burgoyne on that occasion, occasioned by one of the Rector's more absurd accusations, provoked Dr Free into a tirade: 'There', exclaimed Free, 'see how he laughs; the man laughs at what he has done!'[36]

Free's subsequent appeal against that sentence was yet one more frustration for Burgoyne, who reported in December to his daughter Elizabeth (Bess) that 'The wretch has appealed to the Delegates as his dernier resort'. Burgoyne revealed that he had asked Robert Peel, then Home Secretary, to get the Lord Chancellor to set an early date for the hearing. He confessed to Bess, 'I shall be heartily glad when this troublesome business is concluded', adding, 'I believe few people would have persevered in it so long as I have done'.[37]

Burgoyne was also in Sutton in the early months of 1830, not only engineering Free's departure but also writing the first of his two pamphlets on the affair. In addition he set about refurbishing the church and churchyard. This brought him into conflict with the Lord of the Manor, his great-nephew Sir John Burgoyne, who, Montagu complained, tried to 'prevent my doing anything in the Church or Churchyard'. He appealed to the Bishop of Lincoln for support 'which I hope may have some effect on the ignorant Lord of the Manor whom I am ashamed to call the Son of my Nephew'.[38]

Montagu Burgoyne was apparently attempting to repair the seating in the church, and he had also taken the turf off the churchyard as a prelude to planting shrubs. The quarrel with his great-nephew had reached the stage, Archdeacon Bonney reported, where Sir

36 *The Times*, 16 June 1829, p. 3.
37 Northumberland Record Office, Newcastle [hereafter NRO], 2BK Misc., 10 December 1829.
38 LA, B5/7/2/12.

John Burgoyne was threatening to 'turn out' any tenant who assisted his great-uncle in the repairs, and the Constable had taken into custody those who were working in the churchyard. Montagu Burgoyne was certainly stretching his authority as Churchwarden: he had, for example, dismissed the reigning Parish Clerk, probably William Bunting, and appointed a successor, actions that the Archdeacon warned him exceeded his powers. Bonney warned him also that the turf was part of the Rector's freehold and that 'no person could break it or order it to be broken, except for the burial of an Inhabitant'.[39] Work within the church was not confined to the seats, since a gallery, organ and stove appear also to have been introduced at this time by Montagu Burgoyne.[40]

The parishioners of Sutton had several reasons, therefore, to be grateful to Montagu Burgoyne. Not only did he get rid of their hated Rector, he also improved their parish church. Nevertheless, he appears to have left Sutton in 1830, glad perhaps to abandon the great-nephew he disliked so much. Thereafter he flitted largely between his house in London and apartments in Brighton, his wife not caring much for Sheen Lodge, their house in Surrey. His domestic life resounded with the delight they obtained from the company of their grandchildren, punctuated with occasional anxieties about his wife's health. But both he and his wife were heartbroken when Elizabeth, their sole surviving child, died in 1833, only for that calamity to be followed by the death of a granddaughter in 1835. Burgoyne's grief on that occasion is vividly expressed in the letter he wrote to his son-in-law, Colonel Christopher Blackett:

39 LA, B5/7/2/14.
40 LA, B5/7/2/15. 'The conclusion I draw from Sir John Burgoyne's letter', wrote Bonney to the Bishop of Lincoln in April 1830, 'is not in favour of his Great Uncle, and under all circumstances I consider the introduction of these things into the Church without authority, either of the parishioners or Ordinary, highly indiscreet and irregular.'

We have indeed had a house of mourning, and I am sure you will wish to know how my poor wife does, and how she bears the severe blow that it has pleased God to visit her with. It has indeed been very severe. There never was such a little Idol. I can hardly see which of the two suffered the most. What made our suffering more severe was that we had great reason to hope to save the dear little angel. You may believe that every human means was used to save her, but a turn took place and she is gone to her dear Mother.[41]

Before this his energies and charitable instincts had continued to seek outlets. A pamphlet of 1829 reveals him as a passionate advocate of education, but for education of a severely practical kind. He deplored the ways in which children were being over-educated in schools, so that their expectations were raised beyond the limited employment possibilities open to them. This created problems for boys, but, as he wrote, 'The situation of the females is still more to be deplored'. One wonders whether he had the fate of some of Dr Free's housekeepers in mind when he wrote:

unaccustomed to works of labour, and the menial offices of housewifery, they are unwilling to employ their hands to such low employments; they expect higher situations, and finding them not, they at last fall a prey to vice and misery.[42]

In 1829 he established a school in Potton, and efforts to fund 'Schools of Industry' modelled on those at Brighton and at Potton continued to occupy him for several years thereafter. He solicited support from the Duke of Richmond in 1833 for the Brighton school, the object of which 'was to combine habits of industry with the education of the children of the Poor'. There boys were taught to make and mend clothes, shoes and hats, and learn 'to qualify themselves as servants by cleaning shoes and knives and forks'. They

41 NRO, 2BK Personal, box 6, 15 June 1835.
42 Montagu Burgoyne, *An Address to the Governors and Directors of the Public Charity Schools, Pointing Out Some Defects and Suggesting Remedies* (London, 1829), p. 3.

were also instructed in the practicalities of agriculture and gardening, whilst the girls were occupied 'in washing and every sort of needle work'. The Duke duly subscribed the £5 asked of him.[43]

In the early 1830s he devoted himself to various schemes to provide allotments for the poor. He was 'anxious to see the Labouring Poor Man have some interest in the soil, by cultivating for himself and family a small portion of land'.[44] He boasted to the Duke of Richmond in 1832 that he had 'tamed and tranquillised the Parish of Potton by establishing near one hundred allotments'. These, he thought, exceeded those he had previously established in Sheen.[45] He was also a Vice-President of the 'Labouring Poor's Society', an organisation dedicated to relieving the poor by the provision of such allotments.[46] At the age of eighty-two he was writing letters to the *Brighton Herald* deploring those who thought that the 'horrid and outrageous acts of the discontented poor' could be prevented 'by offering great rewards for detection and severity of punishment', and urging instead 'the cultivation of waste lands', such as Epping Forest, and 'the providing better habitations for the poor'.[47]

Burgoyne continued also to involve himself with attempts to improve the lot of poor Irish immigrants in London. These, as we have seen, began as early as 1814 when he played an active part in establish a subscription fund for those dwelling in Calmel Buildings.[48] Whatever the improvements that derived from this were, they did not last long. Writing to the Duke of Richmond in 1831,

---

43 *Huntingdon, Bedford and Peterborough Gazette*, 13 June 1829, p. 3; West Sussex Record Office [hereafter WSRO], MS Goodwood 1463, fol. 485; 1464, fol. 514.

44 See his *A Letter to the Right Honorable the Lord Duncannon and the Lords Commissioners of His Majesty's Woods and Forests* (London, 1831), p. iii.

45 WSRO, MS Goodwood 1461, fol. 137. These continuing interests in Potton explain why his second Dr Free pamphlet was completed there in May 1831.

46 Ibid., fol. 150.

47 WSRO, MS Goodwood 1473, fol. 211.

48 See above, Chapter 4, p. 62.

he related the wretchedness of the many thousands of Irish immigrants living in London. Those dwelling in a tenement block near to Portman Square were again singled out: 'Nothing in the worst part of Ireland', he wrote, 'can exceed it in dirt and wretchedness.' He warned the Duke of the risks to public health: 'There is quite as much danger of Typhous fever as of the Cholera.' Burgoyne's concern was not simply due to the proximity of this squalor to his own house in Gloucester Place: the miserable situation of the Irish poor in London was clearly another of his long-standing interests.[49] Indeed in 1820 he addressed a public letter to the Chairman of the Commons Committee on the Poor Laws, complaining about the ways in which the Irish poor in London were being discriminated against by legislation introduced the year before:

> The inconvenience of the number of Irish flocking to this Country has long been felt and might have been prevented; but let it be remembered, that there was once a time when we were glad to receive them to fight our battles, build our houses and pave our streets: if they are now become a nuisance more than an assistance, let us make use of any other method, than starvation, to get rid of them.[50]

Here was a genuine humanitarian voice.

The lives of Montagu Burgoyne and of Edward Drax Free thus pursued very different courses. Burgoyne was far from being a radical: his view of society was an old-fashioned patrician one that recognised both social inequalities and reciprocal social obligations and responsibilities. Throughout his life he dedicated a considerable amount of time and energy to improving the lot of those less fortunate than himself. There are aspects of his character that grate, such as his obsequiousness when addressing the aristocracy, but we

---

49 WSRO, MS Goodwood 1451, fol. 337.
50 Montagu Burgoyne, *A Letter to the Right Hon. Sturges Bourne, M.P., Esq., on the Subject of the Removal of the Irish, by the 59th Geo. III. Cap. xii, Sec. 33* (London, 1820).

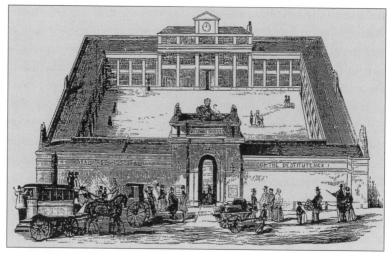

10. The Royal Free Hospital (*Archives Department, Royal Free Hospital*)

should remember that he was a younger son who owed his wealth to a cousin and patron, Lord North, and that he also pursued charitable objectives in which such patronage was very important. He was a stickler for 'duty': army officers should reinforce the King's Regulations; freeholders should do their duty by voting independently and responsibly; and Churchwardens should do theirs by upholding religion and morality.

Dr Free, in contrast, not only neglected his duties, but he seemed intent only on improving his own situation, frequently at the expense of his fellow men and women. Perhaps always more than a little paranoid, he became by the end a sadly deluded creature. If virtue had any rewards, however, they included greater longevity: Burgoyne survived to the age of eighty-five, dying peaceably in his own home at East Sheen. Free's life was somewhat shorter and his end very different. He died at the age of seventy-eight and his death, perhaps fittingly, was sudden and violent.

An inquest held at the Royal Free Hospital, in Gray's Inn Road, London, established that on 16 February 1843 Edward Rolls, of the firm of Rolls and Company, varnish manufacturers of the Old

Kent Road, was driving a chaise up Gray's Inn Lane when a wheel detached itself from his vehicle, Rolls was thrown out and the horse bolted, eventually dashing the chaise against a passing coal wagon. Somewhere in this chain of events, Dr Free was knocked down and injured. He was taken in an unconscious state to the nearby Royal Free Hospital, examined by the house-surgeon, who found two head wounds, and was treated for concussion. Ellen Lee, one of his nurses, said that in the hours that followed he sometimes struggled to speak but she could not make out what he was saying. Perhaps it was just as well: knowing Dr Free, he was either sexually propositioning her, threatening litigation or enquiring of St Peter whether there was an appeal to higher authority. He died at two o'clock the following morning. The Coroner's jury returned a verdict of accidental death.[51]

51 *The Times*, 21 February 1843.

7

Epilogue

NEWS of Dr Free's misdeeds periodically hit 'the public prints', as the Rector complained, especially after 1825 when the Articles exhibited against him were eventually admitted in the Court of Arches, though the long duration of the case meant that *The Times*, for example, had to keep reminding its readers of the precise nature of the offences with which he was charged. It reported the culminating phases of his trial in detail, however, and in June 1829 devoted a leading article to his successful prosecution.[1]

Thereafter details of the case were perpetuated by Montagu Burgoyne's pamphlets. The first of these was his thirty-page-long *A Letter from Montagu Burgoyne, Esq., Churchwarden of Sutton, to his Brother Churchwardens in the Diocese of Lincoln*, completed in Sutton in April 1830, published in London and priced at a shilling. This began with a piece of self-congratulation and a promise:

> Having at last, after many years of trouble and expence, relieved my native Parish from the misery and spiritual destitution which has been inflicted on them for the last twenty years, by the conduct of their wretched and unfortunate Rector, I take the earliest opportunity, agreeable to my promise, of giving you an account of the Proceedings in this Trial, which, on account of the length of its duration, the grave and heavy charges which it prefers, the obstinacy and subterfuges of the Defendant, the enormous expence

---

1 *The Times*, 26 June 1829, p. 2.

both in the Civil and Common Courts of Law, which the Diocesans have liberally undertaken to defray, is one of the most extraordinary Suits that ever appeared in the Ecclesiastical Courts.

His account of the proceedings was prefaced, however, by the story of how, as Sequestrator, he blockaded the Rectory and eventually took possession of the property, and some obeisances in the direction of the ecclesiastical hierarchy, who, he thought, 'have been most grossly, unjustly, and falsely accused of neglect'. He praised the support he had received from his diocesan officials, Archdeacon Bonney in particular, and he drew attention to the way in which the Bishop of Lincoln had picked up most of the costs of the trial. His account of the trial itself amounted to little more than a reprinting of sections of the Articles presented against Free, omitting for the sake of public decency those that dealt with Maria Mackenzie, Eliza Pierson and 'Indecent Books'. He also printed the two presentments made by William Cooper, the Churchwarden of Sutton to the Archdeacon in 1823; a list of the witnesses called in the Court of Arches; and a bald summary of the frequently interrupted legal processes involved in Free's prosecution. Burgoyne promised his readers a fuller account, to be published with the aid of subscriptions from them, the profits of which were to be used to support the School of Industry that he had recently established at Potton.[2]

'My Subscriptions were many, and the profits would have been considerable', Burgoyne recounted in 1831 when he published a sequel, *A Letter to the Churchwardens of the Diocese of Lincoln*.[3] He explained how he had duly prepared an account of Free's prosecution, 'with much trouble and expence', but 'the recital of some parts of the conduct of the unfortunate and miserable Rector when in print, were so shocking and offensive to the eye of decency, that I was persuaded to withdraw it, and sacrifice the profits of the

---

2 Burgoyne, *A Letter to His Brother Churchwardens* (1830), passim.

3 Completed at Potton in May 1831, and published in London in the same year, priced at one shilling.

publication'.[4] What his readers got instead was a further account of the eviction of Dr Free from the Rectory, and a complaint about his nephew, Sir John Burgoyne, who, it appears, had opposed Montagu's continuation as Churchwarden of Sutton. Montagu Burgoyne professed himself hurt by this treatment, particularly as he had ambitions to curb several nuisances in the village. One was a woman in the workhouse, who 'in the absence of her husband, has had several bastard children, and sets a bad example to all the juvenile females in Sutton'; the other was a May Day feast, established some eight years previously by the late Rector, and 'a scene of drunkenness and debauchery for two or three days'. The pamphlet continued with another round of praise for the clergy, a plea for the toleration of religious dissent, a statement of his personal opposition to tithes and, finally, a plug for the Russell family and for the Reform Bill then under active consideration in Parliament. The choice was, he argued, 'Reform or Revolution'. Mercifully he spared his readers further discourses, as he explained, on 'the mistaken notion of a Superabundant Population; the advantage of Spade Husbandry, and above all, the benefit derived from providing Allotments of Land, for the Labouring Poor', though he urged them to contribute a few pence to his School of Industry at Potton. In this curious pot-pourri Dr Free tended to get overlooked.

The latter's attempts to prosecute the Bishop of Winchester for failing to press his case against St John's brought him periodically back into the public eye, and his death in 1843 was widely reported. *The Times* provided full coverage of the inquest, and the *Gentleman's Magazine* and the *Annual Register* provided brief obituaries. He was remembered for being 'unhappily notorious from proceedings in the ecclesiastical courts', but already, by this stage, the details of his career were clouding. The *Gentleman's Magazine* recorded him as being presented in 1830 to the Rectory of Biggleswade by the Prebendary of Biggleswade in the Cathedral of Lincoln, an error

---

4 Burgoyne, *A Letter to the Churchwardens of the Diocese of Lincoln* (1831), p. 4.

that found its way also into the *Annual Register* and Foster's *Alumni Oxonienses*.[5]

Thereafter the affair was saved for posterity by the law reports and through Coote's printing of the Court of Arches' revised version of the Articles, the route by which I discovered the case.[6] Subsequent historians have made little of it. Dr Free was allotted three pages in Watson's antiquarian 'annals' of the parish and its inhabitants,[7] with his account mostly being culled from Burgoyne's pamphlets, and he was given a mere six lines in Joyce Godber's *History of Bedfordshire*, despite being described by her as 'one of the most unsatisfactory clergy at any time'.[8] A bald, and not entirely accurate, account appeared in 1972. It stated, for example, that Free was presented to Biggleswade in 1830 by the Bishop of Lincoln, an event that is barely conceivable in the light of what had happened in the preceding years.[9] Surprisingly, Frances Knight does not mention the case in a recent article devoted to the disciplining of 'recalcitrant clergy' in the diocese of Lincoln between 1830 and 1845.[10] The fullest, and best, modern account that I have discovered is a short article written by Amphlet Micklewright for *Notes and Queries* in 1971, though even this was based on little more than the published law reports and on Burgoyne's pamphlets.[11]

5   *Gentleman's Magazine*, new series, 19 (1843), part 1, p. 440; *Annual Register*, 1843 (London, 1844), pp. 236–37: Foster, *Alumni Oxonienses*, p. 492. The Vicar of Biggleswade from 1810 to 1840 was E. B. Frere, not E. D. Free.

6   See above, p. xiii.

7   E. W. Watson, 'The Annals of a Country Parish', *Church Quarterly Review*, 86 (1918), pp. 215–48.

8   J. Godber, *History of Bedfordshire, 1066–1888* (Bedford, 1969), p. 455.

9   L. R. Connisbee, 'Some Bedfordshire Clergy of the Past', *Northamptonshire and Bedfordshire Life*, October/November 1972, pp. 25–27.

10 F. Knight, 'Ministering to the Ministers: The Discipline of Recalcitrant Clergy in the Diocese of Lincoln, 1830–1845', *Studies in Church History*, 26 (1989), pp. 357–66.

11 F. A. Amphlet Micklewright, 'Clerical Delinquency in the Early Nineteenth Century: The Case of Dr Free', *Notes and Queries*, May 1971, pp. 175–83.

This neglect, therefore, looks curiously like a fulfilment of Montagu Burgoyne's plea of 1830: 'May his vices be forgotten'.[12] But is it deserved? Is the whole business simply a sordid story, best treated with that Victorian reserve about sexual matters that clearly helped to confine it to obscurity? It obviously mattered greatly to the individuals who were caught up in it – to Dr Free, to some of his ex-housekeepers, to Montagu Burgoyne who pursued him so remorselessly, and to many of the parishioners of Sutton. But does it have an historical significance transcending its time and locality?

It was, as we have previously noted, Burgoyne's frustration at the slow pace with which the prosecution was proceeding that led him to organise a petition to Parliament in 1825. After reciting a litany of Dr Free's alleged sins, the petitioners pleaded for an amendment to that Act of 1787 to which the Rector had appealed to impede his prosecution.[13] Two years later, in 1827, Burgoyne and his cohorts petitioned again, this time asking for a short Bill enabling the Bishop to 'provide for Divine Worship in the Church 'till the Prosecution of the present Minister Dr Free be concluded, and to enact the same Regulation in all Cases similar to that of Dr Free'.[14] A further petition making the same plea followed in 1828.[15] When eventually in the summer of 1829 the Court of Arches sentenced him to be deprived of his living, *The Times* drew attention to 'the difficulty which has occurred in bringing this man to punishment through the forms of the Ecclesiastical Courts' and it noted that the Earl of Hardwicke had taken the matter up. What appears to have particularly irked Hardwicke was that Free had by his appeal to the High Court of Delegates produced a situation in which, despite being deprived by sentence of the Court of Arches, he could continue to function as Rector of Sutton until the Delegates had actually heard the appeal. The close of the parliamentary

12 Burgoyne, *A Letter to His Brother Churchwardens* (1830), p. 3.
13 See above, pp. 1–2; and *LJ*, 57, pp. 1110–11.
14 *LJ*, 59, p. 444.
15 *CJ*, 83, p. 85.

session halted Hardwicke's attempt to bring in a Bill to amend the ecclesiastical law, but he promised to resume his attempt in the succeeding session to endow the Bishops, or some other authority, with 'the power of removing such profligate and unprincipled clergymen as Dr Free, the rector of Sutton, from their livings'. Lord Lyndhurst, the Lord Chancellor, promised expedition in the hearing of the appeal, and the Duke of Wellington promised assistance for any measure which would bring speedier relief in such cases.[16]

Relief, speedy or otherwise, was not immediately forthcoming, perhaps because thoughts and energies were diverted elsewhere. Parliament became preoccupied with the great issue of constitutional reform and, once Free was evicted from Sutton, Montagu Burgoyne seemed satisfied, and he turned his attention to his various charitable educational and agricultural ventures. An opportunity to press the case for ecclesiastical reforms came, however, with the appointment in 1830 of a Royal Commission on the 'Practice and Jurisdiction of the Ecclesiastical Courts in England and Wales'.

For centuries there had been conflict within and without Parliament between the Common Law, and those laymen sympathetic to it, and the Civil Law and its supporters. In 1532, for example, the House of Commons was presented with a document entitled 'The Supplication of the Commons against the Ordinaries', a document that complained that prelates and other clergy were making 'laws and ordinances concerning temporal things'; that people were being hauled before the ecclesiastical courts without proper cause; that some were being excommunicated and others committed to prison; that all this could happen on flimsy charges, or to people upon their own admissions whilst being questioned under oath; and that the fees charged were excessive, as also were the delays that users of these courts experienced.[17] The 1532 Supplication set

16 *The Times*, 26 June 1829, p. 2; *Huntingdon, Bedford and Peterborough Gazette*, 27 June 1829, p. 4.
17 *English Historical Documents*, v, *1485–1558*, ed. C. H. Williams (London, 1967), pp. 732–76.

the pattern for later criticism, which criticism became a familiar feature of later Parliaments. It was reiterated frequently in every century from the sixteenth to the nineteenth, buttressing a tendency for legal business to be siphoned by statute and precedent from clerical to secular courts. By the early nineteenth century the ecclesiastical tribunals were but a shadow of their former selves, but they retained a profitable probate and tithe business and were still actively adjudicating in defamation and matrimonial suits. This activity was sufficient to provoke continuation of the old complaints, which burst forth whenever a pretext arose.

Such a situation arose in 1812, sparked off in this case by a petition to the Commons from Mary Ann Dix, a minor languishing in gaol for her contumacy in an ecclesiastical court case.[18] Lord Folkestone lectured the Commons on the long history of these courts, before seizing the opportunity to vilify them. Some of them, he stated, were headed by people 'utterly incompetent to discharge their duties'; 'Their charges were exorbitant and intolerable'; and 'the only purpose of these excommunications and imprisonments seemed to be the extortion of exorbitant fees'. Folkestone concluded his lengthy diatribe by requesting 'That a Committee be appointed to enquire into the state of the jurisdiction of the inferior Ecclesiastical Courts, and to consider whether any reformation is necessary to be made therein, and to report their opinion to the House'. Others, such as Sir Samuel Romilly, joined in the plea for an investigation to be mounted.

Distinguished Civilians, such as Sir William Scott (the future Lord Stowell) and Sir John Nicholl mounted a defence of their courts, aided by William Herbert, who argued perceptively that 'The evils complained of in a great measure arose from the jealousy of the courts of common law, in regard to the proceedings of the ecclesiastical courts'. Herbert also complained, however, about the way in which those who held patent rights to appointments in these courts used them to place their sons or other relations in posts,

18 *PD*, 21, cols 99–102.

irrespective of their qualifications. Despite this, criticism was de-flected from the maladministration of these institutions to defects in the ecclesiastical law itself, and Sir William Scott volunteered to bring in a Bill to remedy these defects.[19] Although this Bill was brought in, it came too late for progress to be made in 1812. It had to be reintroduced the following session, and 'An Act for the Better Regulation of Ecclesiastical Courts in England; and the More Easy Recovery of Church Rates and Tithes' was eventually enacted in the summer of 1813.[20] This measure, which discontinued ex-communication as a means of enforcement, replacing it with a new Chancery writ *De contumace capiendo*, and which raised the value-ceilings below which tithe and rate cases could be determined before Justices of the Peace, offered something to both legal camps and appears to have silenced complaint for a while.[21]

Sixteen years later, in 1829, many familiar issues received another parliamentary airing, when Sir John Nicholl brought in a Bill 'to regulate the duties, salaries and emoluments' of those involved in the administration of ecclesiastical justice. Once again critics took the opportunity to complain: 'their proceedings were so expensive', said one, 'that they were closed to all who were not able to make a considerable sacrifice of money'. This was partly due, it was implied, to the monopoly position of the Proctors. They were, said this same critic, 'nests of sinecures which ought to be abolished'. The 'Ecclesiastical Courts called for reform; the stalls of the Augean stable required cleansing', said another.[22]

Such criticism was the background to the appointment in January 1830 of a Royal Commission of enquiry into the practice and jurisdiction of the ecclesiastical courts, a body empowered to dis-cover what processes, and parts of the system, might be continued or improved and what parts suppressed. In framing their questions

19 Ibid., 21, cols 295–319.
20 53 George III, c. 127.
21 *PD*, 23, col. 396; 25, cols 761–62; 26, cols 311–12, 705–8.
22 *PD*, new series, 21, cols 1318–19, 1543–45, 1700–01.

and collecting their evidence the Commissioners clearly had many of the traditional complaints in mind, but they were equally clearly preoccupied with the question of how best to prosecute and remove from office scandalous clerics. Eight years later, the Bishop of Exeter, Henry Philpotts, implied in a debate in the House of Lords that this Ecclesiastical Courts Commission was set up as a direct result of the case of Dr Free being drawn to the attention of the Duke of Wellington.[23]

The Commissioners began in the spring of 1830 to interview witnesses and in their testimonies we can find many references, direct and indirect, to the case of Dr Free.[24] A prominent Civil Lawyer, Dr Joseph Phillimore, drew explicit attention to the case of Dr Free in replying to a question about the way in which appeals to the temporal courts were used to obtain prohibitions against the ecclesiastical courts proceeding with prosecutions. This, he stated, 'was an illustration of the extent to which the proceedings in our Courts could be thwarted and impeded by a reference to extrinsic jurisdictions'. Asked whether any case in a criminal court could be spun out to such a length, Phillimore answered, 'The case mentioned ... arose from several prohibitions, in different stages of the cause, having been applied for in the Court of King's Bench'. The delays experienced in Dr Free's case, he argued, were not the responsibility of the ecclesiastical courts; they arose from the removal of the case to the Common Law courts.[25]

Dr John Dodson, an Advocate in Doctors' Commons, and one who had actually assisted Stephen Lushington in prosecuting Free, clearly had the ex-Rector in mind when he agreed that 'A manifest delinquent may have the means of protracting the proceedings to

---

23 *PD*, 3rd series, 44, col. 611. I refer to this as the Ecclesiastical Courts Commission to distinguish it from the other Ecclesiastical Commissions set up in the period 1832–36: see A. D. Gilbert, *Religion and Society in Industrial England: Church, Chapel and Social Change, 1740–1914* (London, 1976), pp. 128–31.

24 PP, 1831–32, 24, appendix A, minutes of evidence.

25 Ibid., minutes of evidence, pp. 153, 162.

a considerable length, and occasion his adversary a very heavy expense'. He also insisted, as we have previously noted, that there was no great delay in the ecclesiastical court proceedings against Free.[26]

Other witnesses confessed to their unhappiness with the existing procedure for prosecuting delinquent clergymen. The Reverend George Martin, Chancellor of the diocese of Exeter, thought it was 'clearly in many cases inefficient ... the difficulties which surround all such proceedings, the probability of an enormous expense being incurred, accompanied with the probability of failing in the object, must be considered a great difficulty in prosecuting clerks for immorality'.[27] Granville Venables Vernon, Commissary and Vicar-General of the Archbishop of York, also drew attention to the financial impediments to prosecution: 'The difficulty arises', he stated, 'from the uncertainty whether the parish will combine in pursuing redress', and he thought some way might be found to impose the cost upon the church rate of the parish. He agreed, moreover, with his questioner who asked, 'Is it not very desirable, for the sake of both the parish and of the clergy, that there should be a summary mode of proceeding productive of little expense and delay?' Dr Phillimore also agreed with this question but he pointed to one potential difficulty when the objective was 'to divest a person of his freehold' and that was that 'the temporal courts would always be extremely jealous of any course of proceeding, which, in such a case, did not give him a full opportunity of protecting his property and being heard in his defence'.[28]

One of Montagu Burgoyne's pleas was also considered. Dr Dodson was asked whether or not he thought it advisable for a Bishop to be given powers to suspend a clergyman 'charged with an offence which destroyed his influence in the parish' until the case was finally determined. Dodson's instincts were against such a proposal on the

26 Ibid., minutes of evidence, p. 168.
27 Ibid., minutes of evidence, p. 93.
28 Ibid., minutes of evidence, p. 162.

grounds that a man must be presumed innocent until found to be guilty.[29]

Given that the Report of the Ecclesiastical Courts Commission was written by Dr Stephen Lushington, who had assisted in the prosecution of Dr Free in the Court of Arches, this preoccupation with clerical delinquency is not surprising.[30] The Report itself, as distinct from the evidence collected, makes more or less explicit reference to the case, referring to it at one point as 'a peculiar and an extreme case, in which proceedings for a Prohibition were carried on in the Court of King's Bench, and afterwards by a Writ of Error in the House of Lords; and when the question of Prohibition had been decided against the Defendant, the case was carried by Appeal to the Court of Delegates, where the decision of the Court of Arches was ultimately affirmed'. Nor is it surprising that the Report contained specific recommendations 'that there should exist some Tribunal to which the Clergy should be amenable for any open violation of Morality'. Because, the Report continued, of 'Delays and Expenses attendant on the present mode of proceeding', the Commissioners had suggested 'such alterations and amendments in the present Law, as appear to us to be adapted to maintain and enforce the authority and control of the Bishops over their Clergy; and to provide a Form of Proceeding as summary and expeditious as may be consistent with the ends of Justice, and at the same time calculated to spare all unnecessary expense'.[31]

To secure these ends the Commissioners recommended that complaints should initially be laid before the Bishop of the diocese in which the clergyman was beneficed or licensed, with the Bishop being given powers to determine whether or not a prosecution should proceed. He was also to hear the case, helped by one or

29 Ibid., minutes of evidence, pp. 169–70.
30 A brief summary of the Commission's Report, and Lushington's role in framing it, is to be found in S. M. Waddams, *Law, Politics and the Church of England: The Career of Stephen Lushington, 1782–1873* (Cambridge, 1992), pp. 15–21.
31 Ibid., Report, p. 54.

more 'Assessors' who were to be either Advocates in the Court of Arches or barristers of five years' standing.[32] No case was to be started, however, if the offences complained of occurred more than three years before the start of legal proceedings. The Commissioners also pleaded for the repeal of that Act of 1787 which stipulated that suits for fornication had to be instituted within eight months of the offence being committed. Strict timetables were laid down for the serving of Articles and for responses to these Articles. Evidence was to be taken on oath, *viva voce*, and witnesses could be fined for non-attendance. Sentence was to be pronounced by the Bishop and appeals had to be prosecuted within twenty-eight days of the sentence. Either party could appeal and the outcome was to be determined by the Archbishop of the province in which the diocese lay, assisted by one or more of the provincial judges. Bishops were to be given powers to replace clergymen found guilty of serious offences with Curates whilst their appeals were being determined. These recommendations clearly dealt with some, though by no means all, of the complaints evoked by the case of Dr Free, but still contained elements likely to delay speedy resolution of such cases.[33]

Parliaments thereafter witnessed frequent attempts to put the many recommendations of the Ecclesiastical Courts Commissioners onto the statute book. Some of these attempts were successful, such as that Act of 1832 that transferred the hearing of appeals in ecclesiastical cases from the Court of Delegates to the Privy Council.[34] This was a major recommendation of the 1832 Report. It illustrates a tendency for the subject of clerical delinquency to get an airing whenever questions relating to the ecclesiastical courts came up for discussion in Parliament. Hansard reports Lord

---

32 In the diocese of Canterbury, however, the case was to be heard by any one or two of the Bishops of London, Winchester and Rochester; and in the diocese of York by any one or two of the Bishops of Durham, Carlisle and Chester.

33 *PP*, 1831–32, 24, Report, pp. 54–61.

34 2 and 3 William IV, c. 92.

Wynford's reminder to the Lord Chancellor during prior discussion of this measure in July 1832 that:

> It was well known that at present Bishops were subjected to great expense and delay in bringing clergymen to account for any misconduct of which they might be guilty, and that, in consequence of such expense and delay, individuals, who were really a disgrace to the church, had been able to retain their situation for a length of time. Such cases, he was delighted to say, were very few; but at the same time, he hoped that the recommendations of the Ecclesiastical Commissioners would be attended to; and that another Court would be constituted for the purpose, which would be productive of less expense and delay than the present.[35]

A year later, in introducing one of his ecclesiastical courts Bills, Lord Chancellor Brougham drew attention to the defects in the law relating to the prosecution of clerics, alluding 'to one or two cases, which must be fresh in their Lordships' remembrance, which had travelled through the whole of those Courts, and even up to that House'.[36]

Such allusions to the case of the Rector of Sutton were made frequently in parliamentary debates in 1838 and 1839, when it was referred to as both 'an extreme case' and 'a very sufficient illustration of the evils attending upon the old mode of proceeding in the ecclesiastical courts'.[37]

Reforms in this area were delayed not by lack of parliamentary interest or intent but by a sequence of unforeseen events. Several attempts to pass Bills in 1834 were sunk by rapid changes of government.[38] Introducing the Bill of 1836, Lord Chancellor Cottenham drew attention to the 'very exemplary conduct of the great proportion of the distinguished body which constitute the clergy

---

35 *PD*, 3rd series, 14, col. 259.
36 Ibid., 19, col. 612.
37 Ibid., 44, cols 610–11, 615, 619–20; 47, cols 1308, 1336.
38 Ibid., 31, col. 330.

of the Church of England', but he implied that better means had to be provided to deal with the occasional rotten apple than 'by very feeble, expensive, and unsatisfactory proceedings in the ecclesiastical courts'.[39] His Bill proposed to appoint tribunals of nine local clergymen, under the oversight of the Bishop, to try such cases. It passed the Lords but ran into fierce opposition from the country clergy and lapsed in the Commons.[40]

Two years later, in 1838, another attempt was made. This time it was proposed that jurisdiction in these disciplinary matters should be taken away from the Bishops and vested entirely in the Court of Arches, on the grounds that legal talents were thinly spread in the provinces and heavily concentrated in London. 'It was extremely desirable', said the Archbishop of Canterbury, 'that cases of this kind should be heard before a sufficient court, one competent to decide the questions which came before it ... with a bench of advocates who were able to do justice to both parties.'[41] This proposal met a vigorous attack in the Lords, orchestrated by the Bishop of Exeter, who argued that the Bill was 'the greatest blow that ever was struck against the Church of England'. Lord Brougham preferred the earlier Bills, which were closer in spirit to the 1832 Report. He pointed to some of the disadvantages of centralising legal process in the metropolis: 'if the conduct of a curate resident in Wales was called in question the case must be brought up to London; and the same with a poor parson in Cumberland, in Berwick-on-Tweed, or at the Lands-end'. It would be costly also to bring witnesses all the way up to the Court of Arches, where procedures were anyway dilatory, antiquated and consequently likely to put the prosecutors to great expense. Lord Chancellor Cottenham insisted, however, that there was not a single signatory of the 1832 Report who would now be prepared to vote for a Bill putting into effect their original recommendations. Though in favour of the

39 *Quarterly Review*, September–December 1836, 57, pp. 264–65.
40 *PD*, 3rd series, 44, col. 612; 47, col. 1309.
41 Ibid., 44, cols 615–16.

Bill, the Archbishop of Canterbury recommended that its further consideration be postponed.[42]

When the measure, slightly modified, reappeared the following year it was greeted with a flurry of petitions from the clergy, orchestrated by the Bishops of Exeter and Gloucester.[43] Subsequent debates confirmed the existence of major differences between the views of the Bishops of Exeter and Gloucester on one side and the Bishop of London and the Archbishop of Canterbury on the other. The Bill was so amended in committee that the Lord Chancellor disowned it, whilst the Bishop of Exeter averred that 'he had never seen so much trash contained within the four corners of any bill'.[44]

In the event reform did not arrive before 'An Act for Better Enforcing Church Discipline' was passed in August 1840, a measure that was clearly the result of intensive bargaining in committees.[45] In moving its second reading in the Lords, Lord Chancellor Cottenham indicated this by hoping that 'it would reconcile all the differences which had existed on the subject'.[46] It gave Bishops the power to issue commissions to investigate complaints of scandalous behaviour by the clergy of their own dioceses. The commissioners were to examine witnesses to establish whether there was a *prima facie* case for instituting further proceedings. These could follow only if the offences complained of had occurred within the last two years. Moreover, the limitation of eight months in the Act of 1787 was deemed not to apply to spiritual persons. If there was a *prima facie* case then a number of options were available. The Bishop could, with the consent of the accused, move straight to sentencing him. If, however, the accused protested his innocence, then legal proceedings could be set in motion, beginning with Articles drawn

---

42 Ibid., 44, cols 603–31.
43 Ibid., 47, cols 1029–33. The Bishop of Exeter was the leading objector. Chadwick says of him that for thirty years he carried 'Tory principles into every aspect of affairs', Owen Chadwick, *The Victorian Church* (London 1966), p. 25.
44 *PD*, 3rd series, 47, cols 1306–42; 49, cols 765–72.
45 3 and 4 Victoria, c. 86.
46 *PD*, 3rd series, 55, col. 73.

up by an advocate in Doctors' Commons being served upon him. Two weeks or more after service of the Articles the accused or his proxy had to appear before the Bishop to answer the charges levelled against him. Once again, the accused was offered the opportunity of admitting the truth of the charges, permitting the Bishop to move to an immediate sentence. If, however, the accused refused or neglected to appear, or denied the charges, then the Bishop could proceed to try the case and to pass sentence.

In trying the case, the Bishop was to be assisted by three Assessors: one of whom was to be an experienced advocate in the episcopal court, or a Serjeant at Law, or a barrister of at least seven years' standing; and another was to be a Dean of one of his cathedral churches, or his Chancellor, or one of his Archdeacons. A Bishop could also elect not to try the case himself but to send it to the court of appeal of his ecclesiastical province, there to be tried in the normal course of such proceedings. With this exception, how-ever, existing ecclesiastical courts were specifically prohibited from instituting criminal suits against clerics 'for any Offence against the Laws Ecclesiastical'. Bishops were also given powers to prevent accused clerics from performing services whilst their cases were being determined. The accused were given rights of appeal: they could appeal to the Archbishop if the case had been tried by the Bishop, in which case it was to be heard by the court of appeal of the province; and they could appeal to the Queen if the case had been tried by the provincial court of appeal in the first instance, in which case it was to be heard by the Judicial Committee of the Privy Council.

This dog's dinner of a statute was, perhaps fittingly, Dr Free's legacy to posterity. Although he may not have occasioned the appointment of a Royal Commission in 1830, his case undoubtedly shaped its preoccupations, and time and again in the 1830s Parlia-ment was reminded that it should bring into being some better way of prosecuting delinquent clerics. Supporters of the Church of England made light of the problem, insisting that cases of extreme delinquency were very few. The Ecclesiastical Court Commissioners made the point that 'for many years last past, the instances have been very rare in which it has been necessary to resort to judicial proceedings'. There were apparently only fifteen prosecutions for deprivation in twenty-two dioceses of the Province of Canterbury in the five years preceding the appointment of the Commission.[47] This figure was small because there existed escape routes for those accused of gross misbehaviour. As the 1832 Commissioners reported:

> it has come to our knowledge that cases have sometimes occurred, in which Clergymen, who have been charged with immoral conduct, have chosen rather than risk the issue of a suit in the Spiritual Court, either to resign their Benefices, or to leave them to the care of Curates appointed by the Bishop, and to become non-resident, by licence or tacit permission.

The infrequency of prosecutions was also the product of a system in which the costs of prosecution tended to fall upon those initiating the case. George Martin, Chancellor of the diocese of Exeter, made the point succinctly when asked in 1830 whether present modes of proceeding in such cases were satisfactory. 'I think', he replied, 'that it is clearly in many cases inefficient; the difficulties which surround all such proceedings, the probability of an enormous expense being incurred, accompanied with the probability of failing in the object, must be considered a great difficulty in prosecuting clerks for immorality.'[48] The implications are clear: more clerics would have been prosecuted if the risks and costs of prosecution had been lower. The Bishop of Exeter admitted as much in a parliamentary debate in 1836:

> At present it is hardly possible to carry on proceedings against a delinquent clergyman, in consequence of the enormous amount of the costs. If they made the costs extremely light, they might be overwhelmed with the number of applications for proceedings, but at the same time they

47 *PP*, 1831–32, Report, pp. 53, 56; *PD*, 3rd series, 47, col. 1312.
48 *PP*, 1831–32, appendix A, p. 93.

should not be of such magnitude as almost to prevent the possibility of proceeding.[49]

'Since the passing of the the Clergy Discipline Act', wrote Robert Phillimore in 1873, 'various cases of clerks charged with immorality ... have been tried.' 'The number is not large, having regard to the increase of the clergy in modern times', he continued, 'but it is large relatively to cases of the same kind which happened during the interval between the reigns of Elizabeth and our present Queen.' Phillimore ascribed this to 'the increased energy of discipline under the improved state of the ecclesiastical courts, and the introduction of *viva voce* evidence'.[50] Returning to England in 1854, after thirteen years in New Zealand, Bishop Selwyn remarked on 'a great and visible change' in the Church in the interval. 'It is now a very rare thing', he continued, 'to see a careless clergyman, a neglected parish or a desecrated church.' It has been argued that this improvement in clerical standards was real, not an illusion, and that it was partly the product of the Church Discipline Act of 1840.[51] Something more tangible than painful memories for the inhabitants of Sutton, therefore, may have derived from the extraordinary escapades of Dr Edward Drax Free.

49 *PD*, 3rd series, 34, col. 1168.
50 R. Phillimore, *Ecclesiastical Law of the Church of England* (London, 1873), ii, p. 1091.
51 Gilbert, *Religion and Society*, p. 132.

Appendix 1

The Epitaph of Dr John Free

Here lies buried
John Free, D.D.
Of the University of Oxford;
A native of that city;
Of both the father:
For at the time of his decease
There was not an older citizen,
Nor, of the University, a Doctor.
This man lived in vain,
For he laboured in vain!
Desired no more than
The moderate necessaries of life;
But failed to procure even these,
Either for himself or family.
Fifty-three years a public preacher,
A Doctor in Divinity XLIII.
Yet still in vain!
For, when composing this, tho' sunk in years,
He had never obtained a living
That yielded four score pounds *per annum*.
Astonishing!
When told that he was a priest
in the reign of George III.
King of Britain,
And 'Head of the Church' of England.

Faithful as a subject to whose family,
Faithful, even to his own detriment,
Neither was his political fidelity,
Nor were the labours of his ministry,
Crowned with any reward.
Hence may his life be compared
To the growth of a naturally-fertile tree,
That, shaken by perpetual tempests,
Bending to the blast, and at length subdued,
Resigns its life and fruit together,
Just as if originally barren.
Thus it pleased the Great Creator
To bind-up and to untie his work:
'And is it thus,' as says the Psalmist,
'That all the sons of men were formed to err;'
'The victims of deception?'
If this be so,
Then to those low and dark abodes,
The dread of antient credulity,
This earth may well be joined,
A seat of torment;
In which, constantly deceived,
Traversing intricate paths, at every turn
Insidious snares beset us;
And, after the most arduous exertions,
Hope sinks, entirely frustrate.
How cruel!
'Tis past a doubt, we're brought into this world,
Always to suffer something;
And, what amongst men is justly esteemed
The severest punishment,
Amidst sufferings – to die!
Is not this penalty in the extreme,
When death alone, to which we are born,
As the last great stroke of retribution,

Crowns the work?
Ask we, wherefore is it so provided?
For punishment alone?
Come we into this from another life,
Or from another state of Nature?
Peace to enquiries so delicately obtrusive,
Far better left unbroached!
God only can decide,
Where man in vain may boast to know.
Go, Passenger:
You too must tread life's labyrinth:
Think then betimes, and turn to use
The wise King's dark saying,
'Vanity of vanities; all is vanity!'
Of this aphorism,
Its veracity, and its usefulness,
Consult the evidence below;
Who, in the days of his deception,
(His life was such,) observed
The just man perishing in his integrity,
The villain in his guiltiness triumphant.
Set prudent limits then
To integrity, and to knowledge;
For all beyond is danger:
And why should man persist
To self-destruction?

Source: *Gentleman's Magazine*, 61 (London, 1791), p. 1048.

Appendix 2

The Churchwarden's
Presentments of 1823

Office Copy of a Presentment, Number One, made by William Cooper, Churchwarden of Sutton, at the Visitation held in the Parish Church of Saint Paul, in the Town and Archdeaconry of Bedford, on Friday the 24th day of October 1823, before the Worshipful Henry Kaye Bonney, D.D., Archdeacon of Bedord, lawfully constituted.

No. 1. To the Worshipful Henry Kaye Bonney, Clerk D.D., Archdeacon of Bedford, or to his official.

We, the churchwarden, overseer, constable, and parishioners of Sutton, in the county of Bedford, do present, that our rector, the Reverend Dr Free, has been guilty of divers misdemeanors.

First. In demanding a fee for the sacrament of baptism, and refusing to christen children till it was paid at the communion table. A child near two years old has never been christened on that account, Sunday, the 21st January 1821.

Secondly. That he has omitted several times divine service on the Sabbath day, between November 25th 1820, and December 24th 1820, January 28th 1821, December 5th 1819.

Thirdly. That he has purposely and constantly omitted the prayer for the Parliament during their sitting.

Fourthly. That he has converted the church-yard of the parish into a place for foddering cattle, from which large quantities of dung have remained in the church porch for a considerable time, and the grave stones have been beaten down by horses.

Fifthly. That he has turned unwrung swine into the church-yard, and continued to do so after the admonition of the Archdeacon, whereby the ground has been perforated even to the coffins.

Sixthly. That on account of snow he ordered a corps [sic] with a thin wooden coffin to be buried in the inside of the church, viz. John Selby, on the 29th or 30th of January 1814.

Seventhly. That he has refused to permit the churchwarden and parishioners to enter the church to hold vestries.

Eighthly. That he has refused to let the churchwarden have the register unless he paid him one guinea for it. N.B. The chest with the register is always kept in Doctor Free's house.

Ninthly. That he has made disgraceful affrays and disturbances with his parishioners and servants, refusing to pay them their just dues, and has often been cited before the magistrates.

Tenthly. That he has caused the lead to be taken from the roof of the chancel, substituting a slate roof in its place, thereby gaining a considerable pecuniary advantage.

Eleventhly. That he has been absent from the church since the 17th August, on account of a warrant with which the constable endeavoured to arrest him; that the duty of the church has been, during that time, very irregularly performed, the clergyman who attended performing service in two other churches.

Most of the above complaints of Doctor Free's conduct were made in writing by the parish officers to the Right Reverend the Bishop of Lincoln, in January last, and they were repeated verbally to the Archdeacon, on Wednesday the 18th June last.

[Signed]
William Cooper, Churchwarden
William Coxall, Assistant Churchwarden
William Masters, Overseer
Montagu Burgoyne
John Bowyer
Thomas Brown
James Spragu
John Northfield, Constable

Office Copy of a Presentment, Number Two, made by William Cooper, Churchwarden of Sutton, at the Visitation held in the Parish Church of Saint Paul, in the Town and Archdeaconry of Bedford, on Friday the 24th Day of October 1823, before the Worshipful Henry Kaye Bonney, D.D., Archdeacon of Bedford, lawfully constituted.

No. 2. To the Worshipful Henry Kaye Bonney, clerk, D.D., Archdeacon of Bedford, or to his official.

We, the churchwarden, overseer, constable, and parishioners of the parish of Sutton, in the county of Bedford, do present, that Dr Free, our rector, has been guilty of divers gross and heavy misdemeanors.

First. That he has been guilty of inebriety various times.

Secondly. That he has led an immoral and incontinent life, to the scandal of his parishioners, who cannot conscientiously enter the church where he officiates, inasmuch as he has had illegitimate children by three different women during his incumbency, and another woman has declared that she was pregnant by him, and has sworn that she has miscarried, in consequence of ill-treatment received from him.

Thirdly. That he has been guilty of swindling and shop-lifting.

The second charge was presented to the Lord Bishop of the

diocese in January last, and a presentment was also made by the churchwarden to the late Bishop of Lincoln in the year 1814, as far as it relates to a girl of the name of Catharine Siggins, who swore a child to Dr Free, at the town of Hertford, and a copy of her examination was given to the Bishop.

[Signed]
William Cooper, Churchwarden
William Coxall, Assistant Churchwarden
William Masters, Overseer
Montagu Burgoyne
John Bowyer
Thomas Brown
James Spragu
John Northfield, Constable

Source: LPL, H427/55, pp. 10–11.

Appendix 3

An Act to Prevent Frivolous and Vexatious Suits in Ecclesiastical Courts: 27 George III, c. 44, of 1787

Whereas it is expedient to limit the time for the Commencement of certain Suits in the Ecclesiastical Courts: May it therefore please your Majesty that it may be enacted; and be it enacted by the King's Most Excellent Majesty, by and with the Advice and Consent of the Lords Spiritual and Temporal, and Commons, in this present Parliament assembled, and by the Authority of the same, That, from and after the First Day of August One thousand seven hundred and eighty seven, no Suit for defamatory Words shall be commenced in any of the Ecclesiastical Courts within England, Wales or the Town of Berwick upon Tweed, unless the same shall be commenced within Six Calendar Months from the time when such defamatory Words shall have been uttered.

II. And be it further enacted by the Authority aforesaid, That no Suit shall be commenced in any Ecclesiastical Court, for Fornication or Incontinence, or for striking or brawling in any Church or Church Yard, after the Expiration of Eight Calendar Months from the time when such Offence shall have been committed; nor shall any Prosecution be commenced or carried on for Fornication at any time after the Parties offending shall have lawfully intermarried.

Source: *Statutes at Large*, viii,
ed. J. Raithby (London, 1811), p.755.

Appendix 4

The Articles Exhibited against Dr Free in the Court of Arches

[Some sections of this document have – as in the original – a line struck through them. Those with a superscript 1 were 'reformed after prohibition'; those with a superscript 2 were 'rejected before prohibition'].

The Office of the Judge promoted by Montagu Burgoyne, Esquire, against the Reverend Edward Drax Free, Doctor in Divinity.

In the name of God, amen. We John Nicholl, Knight, Doctor of Laws, Official Principal of the Arches Court of Canterbury, lawfully constituted, to you, the Reverend Edward Drax Free, Doctor in Divinity, Rector of the Parish of Sutton, in the county of Bedford, in the archdeaconry and commissaryship of Bedford, in the diocese of Lincoln and province of Canterbury, all and every the heads, positions, articles, and interrogatories touching and concerning ~~your souls health, and~~[1] the lawful correction and reformation of your manners and excesses, and more especially for ~~the crime of fornication or~~[1] incontinence, for profane cursing and swearing, indecent conversation, drunkenness and immorality; for your lewd and profligate life and conversation; for neglect of divine service on divers Sundays, using the porch of the church of the said parish as a stable, and foddering cattle therein, and turning out swine into the churchyard; for refusing the use of the said church for vestry meetings lawfully called; for converting to your own use and profit the lead on the roof of the chancel of the said church; for refusing, and neglecting, and delaying to baptize or christen divers children of your parishioners; for refusing and neglecting to bury sundry corpses; and for requiring illegal fees to be paid to you for baptisms and burials, do, by virtue of our office, at the voluntary promotion of Montagu Burgoyne, Esquire, article and object as follows:

First. We article and object to you, the said Edward Drax Free, that by the ecclesiastical laws, canons, and constitutions of the church of England, all clerks and ministers in holy orders are particularly enjoined and required to be grave, decent, reverend, and orderly in their general deportment and behaviour in every respect, and to abstain from fornication or incontinence, profaneness, drunkenness, lewdness, profligacy, or any other excess whatever, and from being guilty of any indecency themselves, or encouraging the same in others; but that, on the contrary, they are enjoined, at all convenient times, to hear or read some of the Holy Scriptures, or to occupy themselves with some other honest study or exercise, always doing the things which shall appertain to honesty, and endeavouring to profit the church of God, bearing in mind that they ought to excel all others in purity of life, and to be examples to other people, under pain of deprivation of their ecclesiastical benefices, suspension from the exercise of their clerical functions, or such other ecclesiastical punishment or censures as the exigency of the case and the law thereupon may require and authorize, according to the nature and quality of their offences; and this was and is true, public, and notorious, and so much you, the said Edward Drax Free do know, or have heard, and in your conscience believe to be true; and we article and object to you of any other time, place, person or thing, and every thing in this and the subsequent articles contained, jointly and severally.

Second. Also we article and object to you, the said Edward Drax Free, that you were and are a priest or minister in holy orders of the church of England, and that on or about the 6th day of December, in the year of our Lord 1808, you were duly and lawfully admitted and instituted in and to the the said rectory and parish of

Sutton, in the county of Bedford, and that an entry thereof was duly made in the muniment book kept in the Episcopal Registry of the Lord Bishop of Lincoln, at Buckden Palace, for the diocese of Lincoln, and that you were afterwards duly and lawfully inducted into the actual and corporal possession of the said rectory, and for and as the lawful rector of the said rectory and parish you have ever since been, and now are commonly accounted, reputed, and taken to be; and this was and is true, public, and notorious, and we article and object to you as before.

Third. Also we article and object to you, the said Edward Drax Free, that in supply of proof of the premises mentioned in the next preceding article, and to all other intents and purposes in the law whatsoever, the promoter of our office doth exhibit and hereto annex, and prays to be here read and inserted, and taken as part and parcel hereof, a certain paper writing, numbered 1, and doth allege and propound the same to be and contain a true and authentic copy of the act so entered and made in the said muniment book kept in the Episcopal Registry of the Lord Bishop of Lincoln for the said diocese as aforesaid, on your admission and institution in and to the said rectory and parish of Sutton, as mentioned in the next preceding article; that the same has been carefully collated with the original entry now appearing in the said muniment book, and found to agree therewith, and has been signed by Richard Smith, the Deputy Registrar of the said diocese; and that all and singular the contents of the said exhibit were and are true, that all things were had and done as are therein contained, and that 'Edward Drax Free, Clerk, D.D.,' therein mentioned, and you the Reverend Edward Drax Free, Doctor in Divinity, the party accused and complained of in this cause, were and are one and the same person, and not divers, and that the rectory of Sutton therein mentioned, to which you were so admitted and instituted, and the rectory and parish of Sutton, several times mentioned in these articles, was and is one and the same place, and not divers; and this was and is true, public, and notorious, and we article and object to you as before.

Fourth. ~~Also we article and object to you, the said Edward Drax~~
~~Free, that since your institution and induction to the said rectory~~
~~you have led an immoral and incontinent life, and have frequently~~
~~committed the crime of fornication or incontinence; that you have~~
~~been in the habit of keeping one female servant in the said rectory~~
~~house, and of often changing such servant; and that on female~~
~~servants first entering into your service, and coming to reside in~~
~~your said house, you have solicited and urged them to commit~~
~~fornication and incontinence with you; that on some of such servants~~
~~refusing to comply with such your desires, you discharged them~~
~~from your service, and that with others of such servants you formed~~
~~and carried on a criminal intercourse and connection, and they~~
~~continued to live with you in the said house in a state of fornication~~
~~and incontinence for a considerable time together; and this was and~~
~~is true, public, and notorious, and we article and object to you as~~
~~before.~~ [2]

Fifth. Also we article and object to you, the said Edward Drax Free,
that, in the latter end of the year 1810, you engaged Maria Crook,
spinster, as a servant, and that she thereupon entered into your
service, and went to reside in the said rectory house; that you soon
afterwards formed a criminal connection with her, and had the
carnal use and knowledge of her body, ~~and committed the crime~~
~~of fornication or incontinence,~~[1] and that she thereby became pregnant by you; that you continued to carry on such criminal connection during the time she remained in your service, which was
for about six months; that upon her leaving your service she was
pregnant, and afterwards, to wit, in the month of August, 1811,
was delivered of a bastard child in the work-house of the parish of
Saint George, Hanover Square, in the county of Middlesex; ~~that~~
~~you previously urged and endeavoured to prevail on the said Maria~~
~~Crook to make affidavit before a magistrate that she was got with~~
~~child of the said bastard child by one of your labourers, but that~~
~~she refused so to do;~~[2] and that in the month of July, in the said
year 1811, she, the said Maria Crook, made an affidavit before

Philip Neve, Esquire, one of the magistrates of the said county of Middlesex, that she had never been married; that she was with child, and that you were the father of the child or children of which she then went pregnant, and was likely to be born out of lawful matrimony, and to become chargeable to the parish of Saint George, Hanover Square; that the said bastard child died soon after its birth as aforesaid, and that you paid all the expences that had been incurred by the said parish of Saint George, Hanover Square, in the county of Middlesex, in consequence of the said delivery of the said Maria Crook of the said bastard child; and this was and is true, public, and notorious, and we article and object to you as before.

Sixth. Also we article and object to you, the said Edward Drax Free, that in part supply of proof of the premises mentioned and set forth in the next preceding article, and to all other intents and purposes in the law whatsoever, the promoter of our office doth exhibit and hereto annex, and prays to be here read and inserted, and taken as part and parcel hereof, a certain paper writing numbered 2, and doth allege and propound the same to be and contain a true and authentic copy of the affidavit made by the said Maria Crook before Philip Neve, Esquire, one of the magistrates of the county of Middlesex, as mentioned in the next preceding article; that the same has been carefully collated with the original affidavit now remaining in the custody or possession of the committee of the said parish of Saint George, Hanover Square, for the management of the poor of the said parish, called the Poor's Board for the said parish, and found to agree therewith, and the same will be produced at the hearing of this cause; that all and singular the contents of the said exhibit were and are true, and that 'the Reverend Edward Rex Free of Sutton, near Potton, Bedfordshire,' therein mentioned, and you the Reverend Edward Drax Free, Doctor in Divinity, the party accused and complained of in this cause, were and are the same person and not divers, and this was and is true, public, and notorious, and we article and object to you as before.

Seventh. Also we article and object to you, the said Edward Drax Free, that in the latter end of the year 1812, or the beginning of the year 1813, you engaged Catharine Siggins, spinster, as a servant, and she thereupon entered into your service, and went to reside in the said rectory house; that you soon afterwards formed a criminal connection with her, and had the carnal use and knowledge of her body, ~~and committed the crime of fornication or incontinence,~~[1] and she became pregnant by you; that you continued to carry on such criminal connection for several months during the said year 1813; that the said Catharine Siggins left your said service, she being at such time pregnant by you, and was afterwards, to wit, on the 21st day of November in the said year 1813, at Thundridge, in the parish of Thundridge, in the county of Hertford, delivered of a female bastard child; and that on the 26th day of February, in the year 1814, she made an affidavit before John Baron Dickinson, Esquire, one of the magistrates of the said county of Hertford, that she was so delivered of a female bastard child on the said 21st day of November, and that the same was likely to become chargeable to the said parish; and that you did get her with child of the said bastard child; and that an order was thereupon made upon you to pay and allow a certain sum for the support of such child, which was accordingly paid by you for some time, and this was and is true, public, and notorious, and we article and object to you as before.

Eighth. Also we article and object to you, the said Edward Drax Free, that in part supply of proof of the premises mentioned and set forth in the next preceding article, and to all other intents and purposes in the law whatsoever, the promoter of our office doth exhibit and hereto annex, and prays to be here read and inserted, and taken as part and parcel hereof, a certain paper partly printed and partly written, numbered 3, and doth allege and propound the same to be and contain the original affidavit made by the said Catharine Siggins, spinster, before the said John Baron Dickinson, Esquire, one of the magistrates of the said county of Hertford, as mentioned in the next preceding article; that all and singular the contents of the said exhibit were and are true; and that 'the Reverend Edward Drax Free of Sutton, in the county of Bedford,' therein mentioned, and the Reverend Edward Drax Free, Doctor in Divinity, the party accused and complained of in this cause, were and are the same person, and not divers; and that the signature 'J. B. Dickinson' to the certificate on the said affidavit of the same having been taken and signed before him, was and is of the proper handwriting and subscription of the said John Baron Dickinson, Esquire, one of the magistrates of the said county of Hertford, and is so well known and believed to be by divers persons of good credit and reputation, who have seen him write and subscribe his name, and are thereby become well acquainted with his manner and character of handwriting and subscription; and this was and is true, public and notorious, and we article and object to you as before.

Ninth. Also we article and object to you, the said Edward Drax Free, that some time in the beginning of the said year 1814 you engaged Margaret Johnston, spinster, as a servant, and she thereupon entered into your service, and that you soon afterwards formed a criminal connection with her, and had the carnal use and knowledge of her body, ~~and committed the crime of fornication or incontinence,~~[1] and she became pregnant by you; and that in the beginning of the month of August, in the said year 1814, she being then far advanced in her pregnancy, left your said house, and on or about the 14th day of the said month of August was delivered of a child, begotten by you; that some time afterwards she returned to your said service, and that you thereupon renewed your said criminal intercourse and connection with her, and she again became pregnant by you, and that being far advanced in her said pregnancy, she again left your said house, and some time in the month of November 1815 was delivered of another child, begotten by you, and that shortly afterwards she again returned to your said service, and you again renewed your said criminal intercourse and connection with her, and she again became pregnant by you, and that being far advanced in her said pregnancy she again left your said house, and on or about the 24th day of March 1817 was delivered of another child, begotten by you, and that shortly afterwards she again returned to your said service, and you again renewed your criminal intercourse and connection with her; that the said Margaret Johnston was for about five years in your said service, and during such time you carried on such criminal intercourse and connection with her as aforesaid; and this was and is true, public, and notorious, and we article and object to you as before.

Tenth. Also we article and object to you, the said Edward Drax Free, that some time in or about the month of February 1818 you engaged Ann Taylor, widow, as a servant, and she threupon entered into your service, and went to reside in the said rectory house, and that you soon afterwards took indecent liberties with her person, and several times urged her and endeavoured to form a criminal intercourse and connection with her; that she refused to comply with your desires, and resisted your importunities, and remained in your service until the latter end of the year 1822, when she quitted the same; and this was and is true, public, and notorious, and we article and object to you as before.

Eleventh. Also we article and object to you, the said Edward Drax Free, that in the month of December 1822 you engaged Maria Mackenzie, spinster, as a servant, and she thereupon entered into your service, and went to reside in the said rectory house; that you soon afterwards formed a criminal intercourse and connection with her, and had the carnal use and knowledge of her body, ~~and committed the crime of fornication or incontinence,~~[1] and she became pregnant by you; ~~that you had the venereal disease, and communicated the same to her, and that in consequence thereof her health was injured, and she became very ill,~~[2] and in the beginning of the month of May 1823, she being then about three months gone with child by you, was prematurely delivered of such child, and that she thereupon left your said service; ~~that the linen~~

~~worn and used by you during the time aforesaid had the marks and stains usually appearing from the said venereal disease;~~[2] and this was and is true, public, and notorious, and we article and object to you as before.

Twelfth. Also we article and object to you, the said Edward Drax Free, that in the beginning of the month of June, in the said year 1823, you engaged Eliza Pierson, spinster, as a servant, and she thereupon entered into your service, and went to reside at the said rectory-house; that you attempted to take indecent liberties with her person, and urged her and endeavoured to form a criminal intercourse and connection with her; that she refused to comply with your desires, and resisted your importunities, and in consequence of such your conduct and behaviour towards her she did about a week after she so entered your said service quit your said house and service; and this was and is true, public, and notorious, and we article and object to you as before.

Thirteenth. Also we article and object to you, the said Edward Drax Free, that for several years past you have had and kept in the said rectory-house various obscene and indecent books, containing obscene and indecent prints, and particularly an obscene and indecent book, called Aristotle's Master-piece; that you have frequently shown the same to divers persons, and particularly to the said Ann Taylor, Maria Mackenzie, and Eliza Pierson, during the time they respectively resided in your service as aforesaid; that you frequently made use of obscene and indecent language in your conversation, and exposed your person indecently to the said Ann Taylor, Maria Mackenzie, and Eliza Pierson; ~~and that you have declared and made a boast to them respectively, that you had had carnal connection with young girls not more than ten years of age;~~[2] and this was and is true, public, and notorious, and we article and object to you as before.

Fourteenth. Also we article and object to you, the said Edward Drax Free, that for several years past you have addicted yourself to habitual and excessive drinking of wine and spirituous liquors, and particularly rum, so as to be frequently much intoxicated; and that you have also frequently been guilty of the vice of profane cursing and swearing; that you have at various times sworn at your servants and labourers, and made use of much profane language, and many oaths; and this was and is true, public, and notorious, and we article and object to you as before.

Fifteenth. Also we article and object to you, the said Edward Drax Free, that on a Friday in the month of February 1823, about four o'clock in the afternoon, you were intoxicated, and being in the church-yard of the said parish, and a lamb belonging to you having been found dead, you made use of many profane oaths, and swore at James Steers, a man who was then employed by you as a gardener and to look after your farming concerns, and called him a damned stupid fool and a damned thief, which expressions you repeated immediately afterwards, on the same day in your own yard, adjoining the said rectory-house; and this was and is true, public, and notorious, and we article and object to you as before.

Sixteenth. Also we article and object to you, the said Edward Drax Free, that on a day at or about Christmas, in the year 1823, you were much intoxicated, and that on your then coming out of the said rectory-house, you fell down, and on getting up again you went into the church-yard of the said parish, and that both in your said house and in the said church-yard you made use of much profane language, and many oaths; and this was and is true, public, and notorious, and we article and object to you as before.

Seventeenth. Also we article and object to you, the said Edward Drax Free, that the duty which has always been accustomed to be done at the said church on a Sunday has been the morning service and a sermon, and that on Sunday the 5th day of December 1819, you, without just cause or impediment, wholly omitted to perform such service, and we further article and object to you, that without just cause or impediment you wholly omitted to perform divine service in the said church on Sunday the 25th day of November 1820, and also on every Sunday subsequent thereto, until Sunday the 24th day of December following, and that you also omitted to perform any such service on Sunday the 28th day of January 1821, and that on the aforesaid Sundays respectively no divine service whatever was performed in the said church; and this was and is true, public, and notorious, and we article and object to you as before.

Eighteenth. Also we article and object to you, the said Edward Drax Free, that for many years past you have been in the habit of turning swine, horses, and cows into the church-yard of the said parish, and of using the church-porch as a stable, and foddering cattle therein, and that a considerable quantity of dung has in consequence thereof frequently been collected and remained for a long time in such church-porch; that considerable damage has been done to the soil, and many of the grave-stones in the said church-yard have been broken by the said horses, and the ground therein turned up by the swine, and sometimes perforated as low as the coffins therein; that the Reverend the Archdeacon of Bedford, at his parochial visitation held for the said archdeaconry, did, on or about the 18th day of June in the said year 1823, admonish you not to turn swine into the said church-yard in future, but that notwithstanding such admonition, you have continued to turn swine therein as you had done before; and this was and is true, public, and notorious, and we article and object to you as before.

Nineteenth. Also we article and object to you, the said Edward Drax Free, that there are two keys to the doors of the said church, one whereof is kept by you as rector, and the other by the churchwarden of the said parish; that there is an outer door to the chancel of the said church, to which there is only one key, which is in your possession, and that by means of such chancel door you can obtain access to the said church; that vestry meetings for the said parish have been customarily held in the said parish-church, and that at Easter in the year 1821, and at Easter in the year 1823, and also at Easter in the present year 1824, notice was duly given in the said church of vestry meetings to be held for the said parish, and that a short time previous to the times of each of such vestry meetings so to be held, you obtained access to the said church by means of the said chancel door, and bolted the said church door in the inside thereof, and thereby prevented the churchwardens and parishioners from meeting in vestry in the said church, and refused to permit the said church to be opened for the said purpose; and that you have also at other times prevented the said churchwardens and parishioners from entering the said church and holding vestries therein in pursuance of due notice previously given for that purpose; and this was and is true, public, and notorious, and we article and object to you as before.

Twentieth. Also we article and object to you, the said Edward Drax Free, that, in the year 1820, the roof of the chancel of the said church being covered with lead, you, without any lawful authority in that behalf, caused the said roof to be stripped of the lead, and slates to be substituted thereon in its stead; and that you thereupon sold and disposed of such lead, the money arising from which (after paying for such slating) you converted to your own use, and that the same amounted to a considerable sum, over and above the expence of such slates; and this was and is true, public, and notorious, and we article and object to you as before.

Twenty-first. ~~Also we article and object to you, the said Edward Drax Free, that you have frequently refused to baptize or christen children of the parishioners and inhabitants of the said parish, who have been brought to the said church for that purpose, without a sum of money being previously paid to you as a fee for the same; and have thereupon made use of indecent and profane language; and that you have also often refused to perform the funeral service, and to bury corpses of parishioners and inhabitants of the said parish, which have been brought to the said church or church-yard for that purpose (convenient warning having been given you thereof), without a certain sum of money being also previously paid to you as a fee for the same; that the parents of such children being poor,~~

~~the said children have sometimes not been baptized at all, and frequently not until a considerable time afterwards, and not until the sum of money demanded by you as a fee for the same had been paid; and that such corpses have not been buried until the sum of money demanded by you as a fee for the same had been paid to you; and this was and is true, public, and notorious, and we article and object to you as before.~~ [2]

Twenty-second. Also we article and object to you, the said Edward Drax Free, that on Sunday the 21st day of January 1821 the child of Thomas Smith and Ann Smith his wife, parishioners and inhabitants of the said parish, was brought to the said church to be baptized or christened; that you then refused to baptize or christen such child until a sum of money was paid to you for the same; that the said Thomas Smith thereupon paid the sum then so demanded by you; but that having received such sum, you declared that the same was for the baptism of a former child of the said Thomas Smith and Ann Smith, which had been performed by you; and you then demanded a further sum of money for the baptism of the said child then brought to you as aforesaid; that the said Thomas Smith and Ann Smith refusing to pay such further demand, you refused to baptize the said child, and such child was not baptized; and we further article and object to you, that in the month of April or May 1823 the corpse of a child of the said Thomas Smith and of his said wife was brought to the church-yard of the said parish for burial or interment, due notice thereof having been previously given to you; that you then refused to perform the funeral service, and to bury such corpse, until the sum of four shillings, as a fee for such burial, was paid to you; and you then made use of many quarrelsome words; that in consequence of such your refusal the said corpse was kept a considerable time in the said church-yard; that you at last buried the same, and compelled the said Thomas Smith to pay you the fee of four shillings; and this was and is true, public, and notorious, and we article and object to you as before.

Twenty-third. Also we article and object to you, the said Edward

Drax Free, that on a Sunday, in the month of August 1823, a child of James Randall, of the said parish of Sutton, and of Amy Randall, his wife, was brought to the said church to be baptized or christened; that you at first refused to baptize such child, until a sum of money as a fee was paid to you for this same; that the said child was detained some time at the said church, but that you afterwards baptized such child, without a sum of money being paid for the same, but then expressed yourself angrily towards the said Amy Randall, and desired her never to come to the said church again; and this was and is true, public, and notorious, and we article and object to you as before.

Twenty-fourth. Also we article and object to you, the said Edward Drax Free, that a child of John Saville and of [blank] Saville his wife, parishioners and inhabitants of the said parish, died in or about Michaelmas 1820; that on the following Monday application was made to you to bury the corpse of the said child on the following day; that you then declared you were going out, and would not bury the said corpse until the Wednesday following, and made use of profane language; that on the following day, being Tuesday, the corpse of the said child being extremely offensive and unfit to be kept any longer without burial, and a grave for the same being prepared and then ready, application was again made to you at the said rectory-house to bury the said corpse on the same day, being Tuesday, when you again refused; and that the same was not buried until the next day, being Wednesday, in the month of October, in the said year 1820; and this was and is true, public, and notorious, and we article and object to you as before.

Twenty-fifth. Also we article and object to you, the said Edward Drax Free, that in the month of October, in the year 1822, the corpse of a child of Thomas Gurry, and of [blank] Gurry his wife, parishioners and inhabitants of the said parish, was brought to the church-yard of the said parish for burial or interment; and that on the 31st day of December 1822, or 1st day of January 1823, the corpse of a child of William Giddins, and [blank] Giddins his wife, also parishioners and inhabitants of the said parish, was also brought to the said church-yard for burial or interment; and that in the month of July, in the said 1823, the corpse of a child of Thomas Smith, and Ann Smith his wife, also parishioners and inhabitants of the said parish, was also brought to the said church-yard for burial or interment, due notice thereof having been previously given to you on each of such occasions; that you refused to perform the funeral service, and to bury such corpses respectively, until the sum of 4s. for each of such burials or interments was paid to you as a fee for the same; that such sum of money was paid to you accordingly, previous to your performing the funeral service, and burying such corpses; and this was and is true, public, and notorious, and we article and object to you as before.

Twenty-sixth. Also we article and object to you, the said Edward Drax Free, that by such your excesses, and the gross impropriety and immorality of your conduct, in the several preceding articles set forth, you have given great offence to the parishioners and inhabitants of the said parish; and that by reason thereof they have declined generally to attend, and do not attend divine service in the said parish church; and that for a considerable time past the congregation at such service has consisted commonly of one or two poor persons, and of a few poor children only; and this was and is true, public, and notorious, and we article and object to you as before.

Twenty-seventh. Also we article and object to you, the said Edward Drax Free, that at the Michaelmas visitation for the year 1823, held on the 24th day of October 1823, by the said Archdeacon of Bedford, the churchwarden, overseer, constable, and some of the parishioners of the said parish of Sutton made two several presentments to the said Archdeacon or to his official, wherein they presented several of your said excesses and improprieties, and immorality of conduct hereinbefore set forth, and that in supply of proof of the premises, the promoter of our office doth exhibit and hereto annex two paper writings numbered 4 and 5, and doth allege and propound the same to be and contain true and authentic copies of the said two original presentments which are now remaining in the Registry of the said Archdeaconry Court of Bedford; that the same have been carefully collated with the said two original presentments, and agree therewith, and have been signed by Charles Bailey, the Deputy Registrar of the said archdeaconry; and that 'the Reverend Doctor Free' and 'Doctor Free' mentioned in the said exhibit No. 4 as rector of the said parish of Sutton, and 'Doctor Free' also mentioned in the said exhibit No. 5 as rector of the said parish of Sutton, and you the said Edward Drax Free, Doctor in Divinity, the party complained of and accused in this cause, were and are the same person and not divers; and this was and is true, public, and notorious, and we article and object to you as before.

Twenty-eighth. Also we article and object to you, the said Edward Drax Free, that for your aforesaid fornication or incontinence, profane cursing and swearing, indecent conversation, drunkenness, and immorality, lewd and profligate life and conversation, neglect of duty, using the porch of the said church as a stable, and foddering cattle therein, and turning out swine into the church-yard; for refusing the use of the said church for vestry meetings lawfully called; for converting to your own use and profit the lead on the roof of the chancel of the said church; for refusing, and neglecting, and delaying to baptize or christen divers children of your parishioners; for refusing and neglecting to bury sundry corpses, and for requiring illegal fees to be paid to you for baptisms and burials, and other crimes and excesses, you ought to be canonically punished and corrected, and we article and object to you as before.

Twenty-ninth. Also we article and object to you, the said Edward Drax Free, that you are of the parish of Sutton, in the Archdeaconry and Commissaryship of Bedford, in the diocese of Lincoln, and province of Canterbury, and therefore and by reason of the premises and of the letters of request from the Worshipful Richard Smith, Master of Arts, Commissary of the Honourable and Right Reverend Father in God, George, by divine permission Lord Bishop of

Lincoln, in and throughout the whole Archdeaconry of Bedford, in the diocese of Lincoln, lawfully constituted, presented to, and accepted by us in this cause, were and are subject to the jurisdiction of this Court, and we article and object to you as before.

Thirtieth. Also we article and object to you, the said Edward Drax Free, that the said Montagu Burgoyne, the party agent in this cause, hath rightly and duly complained to us the Judge aforesaid, and to this Court, and we article and object to you as before.

Thirty-first. Also we article and object to you, the said Edward Drax Free, that all and singular the premises were and are true, public, and notorious, and thereof there was and is a public voice, fame, and report, of which legal proof being made to us the Judge aforesaid, and to this Court, we will that you the said Edward Drax Free be duly and canonically punished and corrected according to the exigency of the law, and also be condemned in the costs of this suit, made and to be made by and on the part and behalf of the said Montagu Burgoyne, Esquire, the party agent and complainant, and compelled to the due payment thereof by our definitive sentence or final decree to be read and promulged, or made and interposed in this cause; and further that it shall be done and decreed in the premises as shall be lawful and right in this behalf, the benefit of the law being always preserved.

Source: LPL, H427/55, pp. 4–10.

Bibliography

MANUSCRIPTS

BEDFORDSHIRE RECORD OFFICE, Bedford
ABA 6/25
ABC/17
ABCP 391
ABCV 89
LL 17/330/2
M 10/5/164
P 64/13/2/48
P 123/5/1
PUBZ 3/3
QSR 1811/139, 269; 1823/230
WI 315–19

BODLEIAN LIBRARY, Oxford
MS North d 15

BRITISH LIBRARY, London
Additional 34571, 35130

ESSEX RECORD OFFICE, Chelmsford
S/UI/1

HAMPSHIRE RECORD OFFICE, Winchester
Correspondence of Bishop of Winchester with St John's College,
Oxford, 21 M 65/J7

LAMBETH PALACE LIBRARY, London
Fulham Papers (Howley), 9, 16
Court of Arches H427/1–56

LINCOLNSHIRE ARCHIVES, Lincoln
COR B5/7/2/11–18
FB4/140b
NER 1816/12

NORTHUMBERLAND RECORD OFFICE, Newcastle
Blackett of Wylam Papers, 2 BK Miscellaneous and Personal

OXFORDSHIRE ARCHIVES, Oxford
Archdeaconry Papers, c 91
St Giles, Vestry Minute Book

PUBLIC RECORD OFFICE, London
KB 1/46, parts 5 and 6
PRIS 4/50

ST JOHN'S COLLEGE ARCHIVES, Oxford
Registers vii, viii
MSS L10, L11

WEST SUSSEX RECORD OFFICE, Chichester
MSS Goodwood 1451, 1461, 1463, 1464, 1473

WESTMINSTER CITY ARCHIVES, London
St George's Hanover Square:
Baptism Register 6, Burial Register 92
Minutes of the Governors of the Poor, C 392

PRINTED SOURCES

Annual Register for the Year 1836 (London, 1837); *1843* (London, 1844).

Anon., *Proceedings of a General Court Martial, held in Barracks of Dublin, for the Trial of Col. Montague Burgoyne, of the Loyal Essex Regiment of Fencible Cavalry on Charges Preferred against him by Major Crosse, and Captains Bund and Graham of the Same Regiment* (London, 1800).

———, *A Letter to the Freeholders of Essex, Occasioned by a Public Address to Them, Dated the 22nd of May, 1802, and Signed Montagu Burgoyne; by a Brother Freeholder* (London, 1802).

———, *Merchant Taylors' School: Its Origin, History and Present Surroundings* (Oxford, 1929).

Batchelor, T., *General View of the Agriculture of the County of Bedford* (London, 1808).

Brendon, P., *Hawker of Morwenstow* (London, 1975).

Burn, R., *The Ecclesiastical Law* (9th edn, London, 1842).

Burgoyne, M., *A Letter from Montagu Burgoyne, Esquire, of Mark Hall, on the Present State of Public Affairs, and the Representation of the County of Essex* (London, 1808).

———, *A Letter from Montagu Burgoyne, Esq. of Mark Hall, to the Freeholders and Inhabitants of the County of Essex, on the Present State of Public Affairs, and the Pressing Necessity of a Reform in the Commons House of Parliament* (London, 1809).

———, *A Letter to the Right Hon. Sturges Bourne, M.P., Esq., on the Subject of the Removal of the Irish, by the 59th Geo. III. Cap. xii, Sec. 33* (London, 1820).

———, *A Letter to the Governors and Directors of the Public Charity Schools, Pointing out Some Defects and Suggesting Remedies* (London, 1829).

———, *A Letter from Montague Burgoyne, Esq., Churchwarden of Sutton, to his Brother Churchwardens in the Diocese of Lincoln* (London, 1830).

———, *A Letter to the Churchwardens of the Diocese of Lincoln* (London, 1831).

————, *A Letter to the Right Honorable the Lord Duncannon and the Lords Commissioners of his Majesty's Woods and Forests* (London, 1831).

Chadwick, O., *The Victorian Church*, i (London, 1966).

Cirket, A. F., ed., *Samuel Whitbread's Notebooks, 1810–11, 1813–14* (Bedford, 1971).

Collins, I., *Jane Austen and the Clergy* (London and Rio Grande, Ohio, 1994).

Connisbee, L. R., 'Some Bedfordshire Clergy of the Past', *Northamptonshire and Bedfordshire Life*, October/November 1972.

Coombs, H. and P., eds, *Journal of a Somerset Rector* (Oxford, 1984).

Coote, H. C., *The Practice of the Ecclesiastical Courts* (London, 1847).

Costin, W. C., *The History of St John's College, Oxford, 1598–1860* (Oxford, 1958).

Dictionary of National Biography, ed. L. Stephen (London, 1886).

Emmison, F. G., *Guide to the Essex Record Office* (Chelmsford, 1969).

English Reports, vols 4, 6, 108, 162.

Foster, J., *Alumni Oxonienses* (Oxford, 1888).

————, *Oxford Men and Their Colleges* (Oxford and London, 1893).

Free, J., *A Volume of Sermons Preached before the University of Oxford* (London, 1750).

Gentleman's Magazine, 61 (1791), 78 (1808); new series, 5 (1836) and 19 (1843).

Gilbert, A. D., *Religion and Society in Industrial England: Church, Chapel and Social Change, 1740–1914* (London, 1976).

Godber, J., *History of Bedfordshire, 1066–1888* (Bedford, 1969).

Hansard, T. C., *Parliamentary Debates* (London, 1812–)

Hart, E. P., ed., *Merchant Taylors' School Register, 1561–1934* (London, 1936).

House of Commons, *Abstracts of Population Returns for MDCCCXI* (1812).

————, [Census] *Abstract of the Answers and Returns* (1833).

————, *Journals of the House of Commons*.

————, *The Report of the 1832 Royal Commission on the Ecclesiastical Courts* (1832).

House of Lords, *Journal of the House of Lords.*

Knight, F., 'Ministering to the Ministers: The Discipline of Recalcitrant Clergy in the Diocese of Lincoln, 1830–1845', *Studies in Church History*, 26 (1989).

Micklewright, F. A. A., 'Clerical Delinquency in the Early Nineteenth Century: The Case of Dr Free', *Notes and Queries*, May 1971.

Namier, Sir L., and Brooke, J., *The House of Commons* (London, 1964).

Nichols, J., *Literary Anecdotes of the Eighteenth Century* (London, 1812).

Phillimore, R., *Ecclesiastical Law of the Church of England* (London, 1873).

Salter, H. E., ed., *Remarks and Collections of Thomas Hearne*, ix (Oxford, 1914).

Scott, R. F., ed., *Admission to the College of St John the Evangelist in the University of Cambridge*, iv (Cambridge, 1931).

Sutherland, L., 'The Curriculum', in *The History of the University of Oxford:*, v, *The Eighteenth Century*, ed. L. S. Sutherland and L. G. Mitchell (Oxford, 1986).

Venn, J., *Alumni Cantabrigienses* (Cambridge, 1940).

Victoria History of the Counties of England: Bedfordshire, ii (London, 1972).

Waddams, S. M., *Law, Politics and the Church of England: The Career of Stephen Lushington, 1782–1873* (Cambridge, 1982).

Watson, E. W., 'The Annals of a Country Parish', *Church Quarterly Review*, 86 (1918).

Williams, C. H., ed., *English Historical Documents*, v, *1485–1558* (London, 1967).

Index